Bespoke ELA

Bespoke ELA

Innovative Lessons to Spark
Student Engagement

Meredith Dobbs, M.A.

JB JOSSEY-BASS™
A Wiley Brand

Copyright © 2025 by John Wiley & Sons, Inc. All rights reserved, including rights for text and data mining and training of artificial intelligence technologies or similar technologies.

Published by John Wiley & Sons, Inc., Hoboken, New Jersey.
Published simultaneously in Canada.

ISBNs: 9781394308118 (paperback), 9781394308125 (ePub), 9781394308132 (ePDF)

Except as expressly noted below, no part of this publication may be reproduced, stored in a retrieval system, or transmitted in any form or by any means, electronic, mechanical, photocopying, recording, scanning, or otherwise, except as permitted under Section 107 or 108 of the 1976 United States Copyright Act, without either the prior written permission of the Publisher, or authorization through payment of the appropriate per-copy fee to the Copyright Clearance Center, Inc., 222 Rosewood Drive, Danvers, MA 01923, (978) 750-8400, fax (978) 750-4470, or on the web at www.copyright.com. Requests to the Publisher for permission should be addressed to the Permissions Department, John Wiley & Sons, Inc., 111 River Street, Hoboken, NJ 07030, (201) 748-6011, fax (201) 748-6008, or online at http://www.wiley.com/go/permission.

The manufacturer's authorized representative according to the EU General Product Safety Regulation is Wiley-VCH GmbH, Boschstr. 12, 69469 Weinheim, Germany, e-mail: Product_Safety@wiley.com.

Certain pages from this book (except those for which reprint permission must be obtained from the primary sources) are designed for educational/training purposes and may be reproduced. These pages are designated by the appearance of copyright notices at the foot of the page. This free permission is restricted to limited customization of these materials for your organization and the paper reproduction of the materials for educational/training events. It does not allow for systematic or large-scale reproduction, distribution (more than 100 copies per page, per year), transmission, electronic reproduction or inclusion in any publications offered for sale or used for commercial purposes—none of which may be done without prior written permission of the Publisher.

Trademarks: Wiley and the Wiley logo are trademarks or registered trademarks of John Wiley & Sons, Inc. and/or its affiliates in the United States and other countries and may not be used without written permission. All other trademarks are the property of their respective owners. John Wiley & Sons, Inc. is not associated with any product or vendor mentioned in this book.

Limit of Liability/Disclaimer of Warranty: While the publisher and author have used their best efforts in preparing this book, they make no representations or warranties with respect to the accuracy or completeness of the contents of this book and specifically disclaim any implied warranties of merchantability or fitness for a particular purpose. No warranty may be created or extended by sales representatives or written sales materials. The advice and strategies contained herein may not be suitable for your situation. You should consult with a professional where appropriate. Neither the publisher nor author shall be liable for any loss of profit or any other commercial damages, including but not limited to special, incidental, consequential, or other damages. Further, readers should be aware that websites listed in this work may have changed or disappeared between when this work was written and when it is read. Neither the publisher nor authors shall be liable for any loss of profit or any other commercial damages, including but not limited to special, incidental, consequential, or other damages.

For general information on our other products and services, please contact our Customer Care Department within the United States at (800) 762-2974, outside the United States at (317) 572-3993. For product technical support, you can find answers to frequently asked questions or reach us via live chat at https://support.wiley.com.

If you believe you've found a mistake in this book, please bring it to our attention by emailing our reader support team at wileysupport@wiley.com with the subject line "Possible Book Errata Submission."

Wiley also publishes its books in a variety of electronic formats. Some content that appears in print may not be available in electronic formats. For more information about Wiley products, visit our web site at www.wiley.com.

Library of Congress Control Number is Available:

Cover Design: Wiley
Cover Image : © the_burtons/Getty Images
Author Photo by Ben Fry

SKY10117599_061625

To my darling husband, who has supported me through this journey, and to my "little bird" for keeping us singing and laughing every single day.

Contents

	The Innovative ELA Teacher Pack	ix
	Introduction: Innovating in a World of Tradition	xi
CHAPTER 1	Innovative Alternatives to the Traditional Essay	1
CHAPTER 2	Innovative Approaches to Editing and Revision	23
CHAPTER 3	Innovative Writing Activities for the Real World	45
CHAPTER 4	Innovative Discussion Strategies	75
CHAPTER 5	Innovative Literary Activities for Any Novel	95
CHAPTER 6	Innovative Research Projects	135
CHAPTER 7	Innovative Strategies to Gamify the Classroom	163
CHAPTER 8	Innovative Satire Lessons	179
CHAPTER 9	Innovative Writing Prompts	193
	Call to Action: Becoming an Innovative ELA Teacher	203
	References	207
	Acknowledgments	215
	About the Author	217
	Index	219

The Innovative ELA Teacher Pack

50 EXCLUSIVE Resources for Purchasing This Book!

Don't forget to access the Innovative ELA Teacher Pack of 50 FREE and EXCLUSIVE resources through the following QR code. Simply follow the QR code over to the Bespoke ELA website to download all 50 FREE resources that accompany the assignments, lessons, activities, and projects found in this book.

Introduction: Innovating in a World of Tradition

The United States' educational system comes from the Christian origins of our nation, which has had a profound effect on the formation of what we now call English Language Arts (ELA). Although American education has evolved dramatically since its direct ties to the biblical Colonial era, educators continue to strive to overcome outdated customs and practices from that period. Although progress has been made, we still have need for further innovation in ELA. Today's contemporary, plugged-in learners have grown up with technology and are accustomed to instant gratification, which has had a direct impact on work ethic. The assignments I used to give out 20 years ago would not bode well in my classroom today. Many students would struggle with the depth and breadth of the work, not to mention the time and attention it would take to read a lengthy novel and then write a substantial essay. Students today have changed, and ELA education must continue to innovate to meet the needs of today's learners. To grasp why ELA education must continue to innovate, we first need to situate the American education system in the origins of the past. Only by understanding the roots of American education, particularly reading and writing in our case, can we understand the need for further reforms in today's ELA instruction.

The American education system essentially began back in the 1600–1700s when children learned to read and write from their parents or private tutors, if they were wealthy. This early education was dominated by religion, which formed the purpose for literacy as a means for studying The Bible (Mondale and Patton 2001). Many of the early alphabet primers, such as *The New England Primer* from the late 17th century, taught the alphabet through Bible verses and rhymes (Ford 1897). For example, the primer taught the letter *a* with the rhyme, "A: In Adam's fall, we sinned all." For letter *b*, it used the rhyme, "B: Thy life to mend, this Book attend" (Ford 1897). This was the age of Puritanism in New England, and the staunch beliefs of these early colonizers used literacy education to learn about God and the Christian religion (Mondale and Patton 2001).

But as the nation continued to develop, the need for a literate workforce continued to increase. As a result, Massachusetts took the lead in developing the first public schools. In 1647, Massachusetts called for every town of 50 families to have a free, public elementary school and that every town of 100 families should also have a Latin school. The goal of these schools, however, was still based on learning the tenets of Puritan Christianity rather than learning complex, problem-solving skills, and a child's schooling typically ended about the age of ten (Race Forward n.d.). The exception to this were Latin schools, which were aimed at teaching Greek and Latin for the purpose of preparing learners to attend divinity colleges like Harvard (The English High School Association 2021). Nevertheless, in 1820, the very first public high school in our nation opened, Boston English (Race Forward n.d.). This high school was developed for students who were not continuing to divinity school but still needed further education to gain the skills required to be successful in various industries and businesses (The English High School Association 2021).

During this early era of education, reading and writing education began to spread via a common set of textbooks published in 1836 called *The McGuffey's Eclectic Readers* (McGuffey 1857). Created by William Holmes McGuffey, the Readers were divided into six volumes, each corresponding to a particular grade level for first grade through sixth grade. Selling over 120 million copies, The McGuffey Readers were both religious and nonreligious, highly emphasizing moral concepts along with reading comprehension. They taught more Americans to read than any other book of the time. Such scaffolded learning with a built-in grading system helped to standardize reading instruction and ensure that students progressed through increasingly challenging material. For instance, the first reader taught one-syllable words and simple sentences, and the second level taught multisyllabic words and increasingly complex readings. The third and fourth volumes of the readers were like today's middle school education and included reading excerpts from authors such as William Shakespeare and Lord Byron. The McGuffey Readers were different than other textbooks of the time because they used a scaffolded curriculum that integrated spelling, parts of speech, reading comprehension, and vocabulary (Jones 1998).

Later on, Horace Mann in the 1830s led a movement for what came to be called "the Common School Movement" (PBS n.d.). Similar to public schools today, Mann called for secular, common schools funded with public money, that provided *equal* access to all children. Mondale and Patton's (2001) book *School: The Story of American Public Education* points out that these common schools offered consistency by teaching children the same basic skills in all the common schools throughout the state. These concepts still carry over into today's classroom. Mann's philosophy of education also included the belief that education yields "social harmony," peace, and stability (PBS n.d.). His perspective on education underscored its importance in cultivating the peaceful, stable society that he envisioned. As such, he was a key figure in setting up the first institutions for the training of teachers, and he made some of the earliest moves to make teaching a recognized, respected, and upwardly mobile profession. He also contributed substantially to the framework of a more professional and standardized educational system. Horace Mann made a dramatic impact on leading education reforms toward standardization and toward critical thinking.

Nevertheless, this educational methodology could not sustain the quick expansion and development of industrialization and the need for a more literate labor force at the turn of the 20th century as the change in focus turned towards the ability to use knowledge and facts to effectively solve problems instead of the old traditions of rote memorization (Gibbon 2019).

A champion of this shift in education was John Dewey, who became an influential educational philosopher advocating experimental learning from the late 1800s into the early 1900s. As chair of the philosophy and pedagogy department at the University of Chicago during the industrial boom, Dewey witnessed a surge of illiterate immigrants coming into major cities such as Chicago, which led him to push for educational changes. Dewey famously said, "I believe that education is the fundamental method of social progress and reform" (Gibbon 2019). At the time, however, these ideas were considered quite radical. Larry Hickman has said of Dewey, "[He] was loved, honored, vilified, and mocked as perhaps no other major philosopher in American history" (Gibbon 2019). Dewey's pamphlet, *The School and Society*, released in 1899, established his reputation as a man with new, innovative educational ideas. These ideas, along with several other major shifts in thought, contributed to groundbreaking changes in the education system of the United States. Dewey underscored the significance of active learning as opposed to passive absorption. To Dewey, this meant that students needed to be involved in not just attending lectures but also engaging in activities that stimulated critical thinking. Thanks to Dewey and other educational reformers, today, project-based learning has quickly become a standard in education in many school districts. Dewey also placed the spotlight on the pivotal role that a welcoming classroom environment plays in drawing out student engagement and inquiry. Teachers today have taken this concept to further lengths as many teachers have implemented flexible seating and created inviting classroom environments that feel like home. Additionally, Dewey argued that students not only learn how to perform manual labor but also understand how processes like steam engines or looms worked. He likewise opposed upper-class learning that focused on erudite but impractical subjects such as classical languages. Dewey wrote, "The school must represent present life" (Gibbon 2019). In doing so, he called for a practical education aimed at understanding and practicing real-world skills. Given these radical ideas for the time, Dewey was even termed the "second Confucius" in China (Gibbon 2019). Ultimately, John Dewey became a preeminent educational advocate for experiential learning.

As evident, Teaching methods in today's American classrooms have been profoundly influenced by our history. As we move into a future of continuous technological progression, we must make sure that we as teachers evolve with it. We cannot instruct our students to read a book and then expect them to extract deeper meaning from it all on their own. And why would we want to? Why live in the past? The study of ELA has changed significantly from its past focus on reading, writing, grammar, and rhetoric—subjects that were taught mostly through mindless repetition by family members or tutors. Today, we no longer have students who have the patience to sit and read for hours. Due to technological influences, our students expect immediacy, and we can either ignore that fact and watch them flounder and fail, or we can continue to change how we approach teaching fundamental skills. Education needs to continue to evolve to meet the demands of a diverse student population that has grown up plugged into technology with instantaneous access to the world. Student brains have literally been rewired due to technological exposure, and we need to continue to adjust to this new reality through integrating innovative lessons and strategies to prevent our students from falling even further behind.

Student Engagement

Student success in current times hinges on the elusive quality known as "engagement." But what exactly does this mean? It means that we finding ways to spark student interest in what they're learning. We must ignite interest in ways that previous generations never had to consider. If we can accomplish that feat, then we know we have an advantageous formula for improving student interaction with course materials, consequently creating a more meaningful impact on learners. Students also develop much better reasoning and critical thinking skills when they are engaged in a lesson. Research shows us that when we engage learners, they like school much more—and that translates to better class participation, higher success rates in completing work, and more motivation to care about education. Let's look at what the research says.

- The study of engagement and achievement by Fredricks and Brophy published in *The Journal of Educational Psychology* in 2001 tracked a group of middle school students over time. In all instances, students who showed greater engagement in their learning surpassed their classmates in performance on grades and standardized assessments. This study measured engagement through a combination of methods: the students themselves reported on how engaged they were, teachers observed student levels of engagement, and the students' performances in school served as a proxy for how engaged they really were. Taken together, these three methods of measuring engagement allowed for a more wholesome understanding of the part engagement plays in student learning.

- An alternative investigation of the link between student interest and engagement was carried out by Skinner and Connell (1989). They discovered that learners who are interested in a subject are far more likely to be involved in and motivated to accomplish the tasks required of them. This study underscores the importance of not only hooking students with an engaging intro but also nurturing their interest throughout the learning process.

Numerous other studies reflect these same findings, conclusively providing evidence that student engagement matters, so teachers should shape lessons that tap this key ingredient to enhance their motivation and interest in completing assignments.

But how can we do this effectively? First and foremost, evoking emotions is a powerful way to grab interest and make a moment more meaningful and memorable. An article in *Frontiers in Psychology* investigates the link among emotions, learning, and memory processes (Mather and Schoenberg 2017). The authors indicate that experiences associated with high emotional content are much easier to remember than those that are not so charged. They also argue that the strong recall of these emotional events suggests a much deeper level of processing at the time they occurred. This means that we ought to be paying much more attention to the emotional components of the learning experiences we create in our classrooms. To create emotional engagement in the classroom, it's crucial to get to know students on a personal level and develop lessons related to topics that interest them (Parrish 2022). Instead of teaching only the texts we as teachers like, we should consider our students' interests and use that information to build our curriculum. But what does this look like in practice? It involves selecting texts on topics or themes that relate to students' lives. It means celebrating student success and recognizing what they do correctly instead of only dwelling on what they do incorrectly. It means laughing together and creating lessons that students might even call "fun." It also means striking a balance between teacher-directed lessons and student-directed lessons (Parrish 2022). By reaching student emotions in this way, we can build student confidence, and, in turn, student interest in their work.

Secondly, the establishment of student engagement has an important correlational factor: behavior. As teachers, we can have an impact on student behavior and enhance student engagement by fostering a positive classroom climate, which we can achieve by making the classroom's expectations and procedures clear and by building a sense of community within our classrooms (Smith and Yell 2022). By developing a community within the classroom and by creating predictable routines that students can anticipate and follow, we can thwart potential problems with student behavior in many cases. Behavior tells us a lot about student engagement. As teachers, we should interpret a lack of student engagement as a sign to adjust a lesson or unit. When a student acts out in a way that's disruptive to the classroom, it's because of an underlying emotion or attitude. A student may feel confused, stressed, disinterested, or bored. However, poor student behavior may have nothing to do with the class itself but other things going on in a student's life. Knowing the why of student behavior enables us to work on how to better engage students by paying closer attention to their needs and interests to foster engagement.

Thirdly, cognitive engagement involves critical thinking and problem-solving processes, which represent a higher level of cognitive involvement. These skills lead to improved academic performance and a greater depth of understanding (Perkins 2019). When a lesson or activity activates a student's mind, it reveals interest and intrigue that signifies higher-order thinking skills. We can tap into these higher-order skills by giving learners real-life, real-world problems to solve or generate engaging topics for analysis and discussion. Students flourish when faced with a challenge—but only when the challenge ignites student interest.

For example, think about the difference between these two writing assignments: (1) write a letter to your principal to convince him or her to require school uniforms and (2) select a conspiracy theory to investigate and create a website that presents analysis of why conspiracy theories exist. These two assignments clearly have different topics, and it's not surprising that when I asked my students to vote on one, 99% of them voted to investigate a conspiracy theory. By focusing assignments on engaging topics, we can hook students' cognitive interest, which can be a strong motivator for success. As we continue to innovate in ELA, we need to keep these factors in mind.

My Teaching Experience

I began my teaching career straight out of student teaching at a large senior high school in the Dallas, Texas, area. This district used a district-specific curriculum with prescriptive daily lessons that didn't allow much room for adapting to student interest or performance. However, this curriculum style did equip me with the tools to understand the principles of backward design and how to construct daily lessons from the perspective of the end goal. For that, I am eternally thankful. We then moved to the Chicago area where I attended graduate school at Northwestern University and simultaneously taught high school at a private Catholic school. This was my first foray into not having a scripted curriculum and where I learned to build lesson plans from the macro-level capstone project to the micro-level daily lesson plan. It was my sink-or-swim moment, and it was an adjustment. But I was proud of the curriculum I began to develop back then because it focused on skills rather than rote memorization. The long-held traditions of this school were quite palpable, evident in the 200-question memorization semester exams and the lecture podiums present in every classroom—not to mention the desks that were literally bolted to the floor and could not be moved in certain classrooms. However, this experience gave me a front-row seat to witnessing the clash between the older methods of mindless recall and lectures to the more progressive methods of integrating student choice through project-based learning. It highlighted the different ways to approach learning, and I came away with the realization that there are some students who can excel no matter how they are taught but that most students need more engaging practices to motivate them through the material.

After Chicago, we moved to New York City where I had the chance to teach at a public magnet high school called Brooklyn Technical High School, known for its strong mathematics and science programs. This teaching experience added a whole new layer to my development as a teacher with larger class sizes and autonomy in the classroom. This was where I was able to spread my wings and select my own texts and experiment with different ways to implement reading and writing workshop. Additionally, with New York City as my oyster for exploration, it also became my inspiration to create real-world lessons that mattered to students. Some of these projects were a serial killer research paper, a world issue campaign project (inspired by the many advocates I saw on the streets of New York City with their petitions in hand), and a comic book project. I also sponsored the school's geocaching club, which inspired me to create a geocache literary project to reflect the protagonist's journey. I saw what my students were interested in and found ways to integrate their interests into their work. I finally began to see the incredible potential of project-based learning and the importance of tapping student interest to harness engagement and motivation. These new project concepts resonated with my students, and they were excited to approach ELA skills in a whole new way.

After five years of living in Brooklyn and becoming a mother, I decided to take a leave of absence from the classroom to stay home with my daughter until she started kindergarten. During those years, I found myself falling deeper and deeper into my passion for creating innovative ELA lessons to sell on Teachers Pay Teachers (TpT) through my shop Bespoke ELA (`BespokeClassroom.com`). Writing curriculum has always been one of my favorite aspects of teaching because it enables me to be creative and inspires me to rethink how to teach skills in more inventive ways.

From New York, we moved to Miami where I continued my TpT journey and delved more into the innovative aspects of creating engaging units for teachers who were still in the classroom. It was important to me to stay connected to current trends in ELA education so that I could be prepared for when I returned to the classroom. Then, after my daughter turned five, we moved back to the Dallas area (where I'm from), and I returned to the classroom where I have been teaching ever since. For the past six years, I have concentrated on teaching dual credit college courses to high school students along with AP Literature. Dual credit is such a rewarding role because it takes the traditional supports of high school and combines them with the college system, enabling learners to thrive in a much more rigorous academic environment. I feel incredibly fortunate to work with the amazing students I have the privilege of teaching. When I see students graduate high school with college credits under their belts—some even earning associate's degrees—I know that I'm exactly where I'm meant to be.

My School District's Profile

The school where I teach in Dallas County has an extremely diverse student body. In fact, we are proud of our school's diversity and take strides to celebrate our students' backgrounds. Our school continually works to create engaging and dynamic instructional experiences that motivate our group of diverse learners. We have worked hard to close achievement gaps with noticeable progress in student scores over time. This progress correlates to the dedicated efforts of our faculty and staff, who consistently seek out new approaches to enhance learning—including the fact that we are an AVID demonstration school, recognized for effectively implementing the AVID (Advancement Via Individual Determination) program to promote college readiness and academic success for all students. Our high school integrates cutting-edge technology and best practices to guide students toward success. I am grateful to work in an environment that meets its challenges head-on with bold ideas and a desire to experiment with what works best for our school's population. It's this forward-thinking approach that has driven the recent improvements in our students' scores. Many of the strategies in this book are concepts I've developed to motivate and support at-risk students.

xxii Introduction: Innovating in a World of Tradition

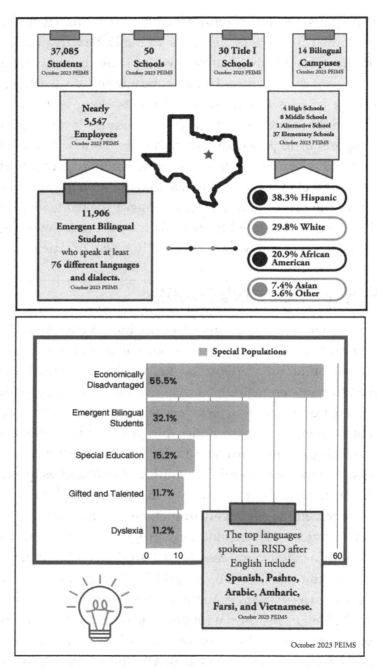

FIGURE I.1 My school's district demographics and information.

Introduction: Innovating in a World of Tradition

See Figure I.1 for information about the high school where I teach in Texas. However, regardless of your school's demographics, the strategies outlined in *Bespoke ELA: Innovative Lessons to Spark Student Engagement* are designed to inspire a student from any background. By including gamification, offering student choice, using dynamic movement, and employing high-interest topics, we can better motivate, encourage, and inspire our students to want to do the work and to want to improve their skills. Thus, these are central components to the lessons found within this book.

It was important to me that *Bespoke ELA: Innovative Lessons to Spark Student Engagement* offer creative resources that teachers could use immediately in their classrooms. With so many books on the market about theories of learning and teaching, I wanted to present something totally different: a compilation of lessons, projects, and assignments that are ready to use in the classroom as soon as tomorrow. The explanations of ideas included in *Bespoke ELA: Innovative Lessons to Spark Student Engagement* make it easy for teachers to cultivate flexibility and adaptability in the classroom, helping students with diverse learning abilities. I've also included 50 FREE printable resources (downloadable on the Bespoke ELA website) that accompany the activities in this book. To access this set of free resources, please scan the following QR code to download the materials. They will help you implement most of the lessons and activities explained here in the book.

CHAPTER ONE

Innovative Alternatives to the Traditional Essay

Essay writing is a cornerstone skill in any English Language Arts (ELA) class. As English teachers, we have experienced the evolution of writing strategies from the traditional five-paragraph essay to a writing workshop model and everything in between. This innovation in our content area carries on into current times as we seek newer and better methods to engage our students in their own writing while targeting the skills we want them to master, such as creating thesis statements organizing ideas, offering evidence, providing commentary, and using proper grammar. The traditional five-paragraph essay is not the only method we can employ to target these same writing skills; there are others with a more exciting twist for student interest. In this chapter, I share alternative options to the traditional essay to motivate our writers without sacrificing skills.

The Infographic Essay

The infographic essay can replace a traditional essay to support visual learners. These graphics offer a succinct way to represent information visually while targeting key writing skills. Assigning an infographic essay also enables students to learn about the basic principles of visual design and layout— relevant skills in today's job market—alongside their analysis. According to Bowdon and Scott (2003), visuals paired with text create "enhanced student engagement" and allow for "the communication of enriched content" (41). Infographic essays can be

FIGURE 1.1 Infographic analyzing a key theme in Shakespeare's play *Macbeth*.

tailored to a variety of essay types from literary analysis to persuasive messages. See Figure 1.1 for an example of a literary analysis infographic. This method fulfills the demands of curriculum standards but also the demand for students to gain a better understanding of the material through visual, creative expression as opposed to the traditional essay.

I've used infographics in so many ways in my classes. During a recent unit on Gothic literature, students created infographics to analyze gothic traits, using images and textual evidence to support an analytical thesis statement about how gothic traits create suspense and tension in a story. They used a template from Canva to construct their infographics and then presented them to small groups and put them on display around the classroom for a gallery walk activity. This approach helped them understand how the specific traits of a genre affect the reader's experience. As an extension, students can use the infographic as an outline for a new essay. Thus, this approach can also act as a visual outline for planning a piece of writing.

However, there are various ways to use infographics across ELA grades and levels. Here are essay prompt options that work for using infographics to supplement or replace a conventional essay entirely.

- **Character Analysis**
  - **Writing task.** Conduct an analysis of the protagonist's character development in a novel. Observe how the character changes from the beginning until the end. How does this character's change communicate the theme of the story? Create an infographic essay that answers this question.

- **Symbolism**
  - **Writing task.** Select a symbol from a literary work. Examine how the symbol communicates the theme of the story. Communicate your analysis through an infographic.

- **Literary Devices**
  - **Writing task.** Explain the use of a literary device in a text (e.g., metaphor, irony, foreshadowing) and how it contributes to the meaning of the work as a whole. Design an infographic to showcase your analysis.

- **Thematic Exploration**
  - **Writing task.** Investigate a key theme of the text. Analyze how literary techniques and/or elements communicate this theme.

- **Historical and Cultural Context**
  - **Writing task.** Investigate the historical and cultural context of a piece of literature and think about its impact on the story's main message. Use an infographic to explain your findings.

- **Author Study**
  - **Writing task.** Investigate an author's life experiences and output of written work. Think about how his or her life events and beliefs influenced his or her body of work. Create an infographic that explores this connection.

These assignments, when transformed into infographics, encourage students to think analytically and creatively about how to represent their analysis using a combination of images and words, making the presentation of information and learning process more interesting and interactive.

Helpful Hint: Have students use QR codes on the infographic to link to related content. They can then use these external sites to learn more about the topic during a gallery walk. Students can also select an infographic from another student or group and use the rubric to assess it, providing feedback to the writer/creator on the strong points as well as areas for improvement.

The Infographic Essay Project targets essential skills in a much more succinct format than a full essay. For instance, we can check the thesis statement overall organization of ideas, and supporting evidence all through the context of an infographic. To add in assessment of commentary, students can present their infographics to the class and explain how each device or quotation supports the thesis statement. Students can also get creative with these, using specific colors to symbolize thematic topics in the text (e.g., a red border could represent murder or destruction and a skull could represent death). Encourage learners to experiment with templates from Canva to find the one that will best convey their ideas. That way, students can focus more on the content and less on the rules for creating an aesthetic layout. Using visuals like the infographic can help students "see" their writing path.

The Photo Essay

The Photo Essay presents another alternative to the traditional essay. This method of writing entails using the artistic form of photography to connect and convey analysis of a text. Students can either select photos or take their own original photos that connect to the main ideas, or what would be the body paragraphs of an essay, to support and prove a thesis statement. Once they have created their photo essays, students can present their essays to the class, explain how the photographs relate to the text, and use textual evidence to prove their analysis. According to Serafini (2014), combining visual and textual elements in classroom projects fosters critical thinking and allows learners to engage with literature in dynamic, multimodal ways. This multimodal approach enables teachers to examine students' understanding and depth of analysis through their careful attention to how they relate the text to photography. Analyzing literature through photography can make the writing process more tangible and relatable to visual learners.

Instead of presenting their photo essays live to the whole class, students can record their analyses as a voiceover in an animated slideshow (like a film) and present their interpretations of a text in a visual and auditory way. When students create recordings of their presentations, other students can watch presentations asynchronously and fill out response guides. This strategy works well with both fiction and nonfiction texts in any unit of study.

Helpful Hint: Instead of relying on found images from the internet, prompt students to capture their own photographs. This added action not only pushes them to the next level of artistic expression but also encourages them to think more deeply about the text. It requires them to stage or find scenes that represent their analysis and take pictures that represent their interpretation.

Try out these prompts for literary analysis photo essays:

- Choose an important literary symbol and create a photo essay that examines its meaning and importance. Use direct quotes from the text to connect each photo with the symbol.

- Choose a complex character from a novel and represent his or her defining character traits through a set of images. Think about the character's background relationships, and internal conflicts. How does this character connect to each image, and what does each image say about the character? Include textual evidence to support claims and weave a narrative about the defining aspects of this character's life and personality.

- Establish a thematic interpretation of a text using visuals and textual evidence. Make a clear connection between the photographs and theme. What do the photos have to say about the theme? What evidence from the text supports the use of photos in establishing a thematic interpretation?

Try out these other prompts for nonfiction photo essays:

- Produce a photographic memoir. Chronicle a life-changing, personal event that affected you in a significant way, depicting it with visuals and words.
- Use your investigative skills to highlight a problem in your community and raise awareness about it. Support your findings with research from credible sources.
- What is your cultural heritage? Conduct research to find out more about your background. Then, present your findings through words and pictures.

Essentially, the Photo Essay Project provides students with a multimedia project that requires similar planning and depth of analysis as a traditional essay. Thesis statements, organization, research, evidence, and commentary are basic writing skills, and photo essays give students the chance to explore these skills through this creative medium. Today's learners will enter a workforce that demands they be proficient in a variety of media forms. According to Hobbs (2011), integrating multimedia projects into the classroom prepares students for the demands of the present workplace by teaching them to critically analyze and create media for various purposes. Thus, multimedia projects such as the photo essay enable instructors to teach important skills that are relevant beyond the classroom.

Of all the alternative writing assignments I've tried, the Photo Essay truly resonates with students. They get excited when they can make connections to photos and even more excited when they get to take their own photos. By allowing students to be creative and make choices, they tend to engage with the assignment and the skills so much more. It's a win-win!

The Paragraph Portfolio

The Paragraph Portfolio Project involves creating a portfolio of paragraphs in lieu of one, long essay. The portfolio empowers students to sharpen writing skills while focusing on shorter pieces of writing that tend to be more accessible and far less intimidating than a lengthy essay. In fact, the Paragraph Portfolio Project serves as an effective strategy to help students build up the stamina to write full-length essays.

There are various approaches to constructing this portfolio project, but one effective method is for students to use their journals throughout the semester, building a collection of paragraph options to include in their final portfolio. Focus on giving journal prompts that require responses with textual evidence and commentary. This will give enough substance to start the writing process as learners compile their portfolios (Dobbs 2018). Example prompts include the following:

- What is the most defining characteristic of the main character? Explain with textual evidence.
- Predict what happens next in the story based on the reading thus far. Use textual evidence to support the prediction.
- How does the simile (or other device) create meaning in the passage? Explain with textual evidence.
- Find one symbol from the reading and explain what it means using textual evidence.
- Describe the tone of the passage. What is the tone and how does it affect the meaning? Explain with textual evidence.

After students have drafted a few paragraph journals, they can begin writing workshop mini lessons that target skills such as writing topic sentences, blending evidence, and crafting commentary. Give students time to workshop their paragraph drafts throughout the semester so that when it comes time to compile the entire portfolio at the end of the semester, they will have already completed editing and revision exercises on select paragraphs. Consider allowing them to choose which paragraphs to work on during writing workshop time and which paragraphs to submit in the final portfolio. Alternatively, strike a balance between student-selected paragraphs and teacher-selected paragraphs as best fits the needs of your students.

For submitting their paragraph portfolios, students can turn in a physical folder or create an online repository for them such as a Google folder or a built-in portfolio component of a learning management system such as Schoology. I prefer to give each student a file folder to turn in printed versions of their paragraphs because I find it easier to grade this way. However, we have printing capabilities at our school that others may not have, so online portfolios can work just as well.

When it comes to grading the portfolio, I find it less daunting and more manageable to audit each one instead of grading every single paragraph (Dobbs 2018). A portfolio audit enables me to hold students accountable without having to grade every piece of paper. But what is a "grade audit"? As teachers, we cannot grade every single piece of paper. There are too many of students and only one of us, which can lead to hours upon hours of grading written work. Instead, I audit the portfolio by requiring a set number of paragraphs (e.g., six to ten is a typical range), and their grade comes from two main components: completion of all paragraphs in the correct format and the quality of a small number of paragraphs (e.g., two to four is a usual amount). Essentially, this means that I only end up assessing between two and four paragraphs instead of reading all 6–10. I allow students to select some paragraphs for me to grade and then I select the others at random. This enables me to maintain accountability without drowning in papers. Let me show you an example assignment breakdown of how this works:

- Students must include eight paragraphs (or however many you would like to assign) in the paragraph portfolio.
- Each paragraph should include a topic sentence, two to three pieces of textual evidence embedded into student writing, commentary or explanations of evidence, and a concluding sentence.
- Each paragraph should appear on its own page with its own MLA format and a Works Cited page.
- Students submit the eight paragraphs in a file folder and highlight and label the targeted writing skills mentioned above.
- Out of the eight paragraphs, I will grade four for quality and the rest for completion. Students select two of their best paragraphs for me to grade, and I select the other two paragraphs at random.
- Sixty percent of the grade comes from completing all eight paragraphs in proper MLA format. The other 40% of the grade comes from the quality of the four that I assess for targeted writing skills.

This forms the basis of audit grading. These numbers can be changed around depending on your student group. For instance, in an advanced class, I might require students to include 10 paragraphs in the portfolio and then assess 6 of the 10 for quality. For other classes, I might require six paragraphs, two for me to grade for quality and the rest for completion. It depends on the class and how best to meet student needs.

Each year, my students report that the Paragraph Portfolio Project taught them how to write. They appreciate that the paragraphs make writing workshop less intimidating and more approachable when working on specific writing skills. Thus, the Paragraph Portfolio Project has become a staple in my curriculum. Targeting skills in shorter chunks of writing helps build student confidence and encourages them to take more risks in their writing. It also prepares them to write longer, more developed essays by ensuring that they have the paragraph-writing skills necessary to handle a more lengthy writing challenge (Dobbs 2018).

Flash Presentation

A Flash Presentation means fast. It consists of a concise and focused presentation format in which the presenter has 30 seconds to present each slide for a total of six slides, resulting in a presentation time of about three minutes. Note that times can be changed as needed to fit the assignment and the student group. This condensed format requires students to be clear, organized, and prepared when they present. It is ironic that by giving students more time to prepare can actually cause more procrastination and less organization. The same concept applies to writing, too. Sometimes, limiting the amount of writing can actually make for better writing because it forces the writer to strip down the message to its key points. According to Zinsser (2006), brevity and clarity are important skills in communication, helping students refine their thinking and focus on what truly matters. Time limits can do the same by helping them cut out the fluff and get to the heart of their message.

To use the Flash Presentation for assessing writing skills outside the context of an essay, teachers can require the following skills in the presentation for assessment:

- **Thesis statement.** Students begin their presentations with a clearly stated, focused thesis statement just like in a traditional essay.
- **Organization of ideas.** Then students arrange their concepts in a coherent sequence throughout the presentation. Each part should denote a specific point along with evidence that substantiates the thesis statement. This part of the presentation parallels the organizational skills one must use to write an effective essay.
- **Research and evidence.** Similar to an essay, students also need to support the thesis statement with evidence during the presentation.

They can select relevant quotes, data, and/or examples from the text or research to share, but writers must select focused chunks of text for the presentation given the time constraints. Using this strategy, students can't merely throw in a long passage just to take up space in an essay. They must focus in on precise words, phrases, and quotations that best support their claims.

- **Analysis and commentary.** Students can also explain how the evidence supports their thesis and what it reveals about other elements such as characters, conflicts, and symbols in the text. If it is a nonfiction presentation about an issue, students can use evidence from credible sources in lieu of literary elements. Again, because of the time limit, students need to come well-rehearsed and prepared to share their commentary in a clear and concise format. Similar to the commentary in an essay, this component presents analysis—just in a much shorter presentation style.

- **Concise writing.** The Flash Presentation format encourages students to be organized and prepared. They have only 30 seconds per slide, so they must simplify their analysis into its most essential parts. This brevity helps them practice being succinct while avoiding unnecessary filler information—another key skill in essay writing.

Helpful Hint: I set up a large digital stopwatch at the back of the room so that students can see it while they present. This helps them stay on time throughout the presentation. I do allow grace time, especially at first, but students get better at flash presentations the more they do them. And the more they do them, the more they like them because they are straight and to the point.

The Flash Presentation enables teachers to assess students in a fast and effective format while also checking for key writing skills. This technique can be used for both fiction and nonfiction texts. Whether students present a character analysis or an issue-based public service announcement, the Flash Presentation provides the means of delivering information quickly and efficiently, which works for anything we do in ELA.

Museum Artifact Presentation

The Museum Artifact Presentation gives students a tactile way to build critical thinking and writing skills. It is a way for learners to showcase analysis by making connections. For this presentation assignment, students choose an artifact that connects to a literary text and then explain how the artifact advances further understanding of literary elements and/or techniques such as themes, characters, or symbols. The artifacts assist students in brainstorming thematic topics, ultimately guiding them to craft a thematic thesis statement that connects the artifact to the literary work and uses it as a foundation for analysis. As Kelly Gallagher (2004) reminds us, when we engage students in innovative, hands-on activities, we give them the chance to be intellectually inquisitive, and as a result, they often surprise us with the insights they uncover. Sometimes, learners struggle with abstract ideas. This project helps students generate thematic topics by starting with tangible objects that they can hold in their hands and use as a guide to the big, universal, thematic ideas.

For example, in a novel study unit on *The Great Gatsby*, items could include a flapper dress, a golf club, a green light a pair of eyeglasses, a string of pearls, a yellow toy car, a party invitation, a map of New York City and Long Island, and so on. Groups can work to analyze how each item connects to a thematic idea to inspire a thematic thesis statement. For instance, the thesis statement for the flapper dress might be something like: "The flapper dress, as an icon of the Jazz Age, serves as a symbol of the illusion of freedom and prosperity in *The Great Gatsby* and ultimately reflects the shallowness of Daisy Buchanan." Consider these other artifacts for popular secondary texts:

- A red balloon for *The House on Mango Street* by Sandra Cisneros
- An astronomy book for *Wonder* by R. J. Palacio
- A conch shell for *The Lord of the Flies* by William Golding

- A crochet hook and yarn for *Esperanza Rising* by Pam Muñoz Ryan
- A small shovel for *Holes* by Louis Sachar
- A bow for *The Odyssey* by Homer
- A red apple for *The Giver* by Lois Lowry
- A letter for *Pride and Prejudice* by Jane Austen

Helpful Hint: Allow students to choose artifacts that speak to their interpretations of the text because student choice can increase engagement and motivation. Alternatively, consider having them create their own artifacts, or allow students to choose a few pieces to put on display in a literary museum. This project can be short and simple or more involved, depending on the curriculum and needs of a class.

The number of artifacts to require for this assignment can vary. Typically, I require students to present two to three artifacts that all connect to the same overall idea. Once students have selected their artifacts, they must explore how each one connects to the text by finding textual evidence to support a thematic connection. They also conduct research about each artifact to see if anything from the research helps to enlighten thematic meaning. For a flapper dress, students could investigate fashions from the 1920s, paying particular attention to the popularity of the flapper dress and its representation of free expression. Through research and textual evidence, students can begin to view the dress as a symbolic artifact representing both the illusion of freedom promised by the American Dream and the carefully curated facade it required. By integrating evidence into their presentations—from the text and other credible sources—students can enhance their ability to gather, evaluate, and integrate evidence to support a thematic claim.

As far as using this project to assess writing skills, consider having students turn in a developed outline of their artifact presentations.

The outline gives teachers a chance to assess the thesis statement, organization, use of evidence, and analysis. As students present, I follow along with the outline and check for targeted writing skills. The rest of the class can also assess presentations as they listen and evaluate the effectiveness of each overall argument.

Extensions and enrichment ideas for the Museum Artifact Project include the following:

- Construct a museum exhibit to put on display for the whole school in the library, hallway, or other community space.
- Focus on how different characters perceive the artifact to explore perspective.
- Use creativity to invent a backstory for the artifact to examine where it might have come from and how a character in the novel could have acquired it.
- Rework a scene in which the artifact changes the course of the novel.
- Create an original artifact, incorporating any pertinent details, colors, or symbols from the text that would signify the artifact's importance.
- Write a diary entry, letter, or monologue from the perspective of a character who reflects on the importance of the artifact.

Through various pathways and choices in the presentation of the Museum Artifact Project, teachers can guide students to explore the symbolism of artifacts, ensuring engagement with the material at an appropriately challenging level. According to Thomas C. Foster's (2014) book *How to Read Literature Like a Professor*, "Everything is a symbol of something, it seems, until proven otherwise." Embracing the symbolic nature of artifacts encourages students to think critically about the deeper meanings within literature and the world around them.

Literary Quilt Project

The Literary Quilt Project presents another interactive and visual opportunity to analyze a literary work while sharpening both writing and critical thinking abilities. For this project, students can communicate their understanding of a literary work by creating a quilt (out of paper or fabric—or even online) that presents their analysis of a text. This process encourages both presenters and listeners to show their understanding of a text. Creating a story quilt requires collaboration as students share their interpretations of a text, decide what to put on the quilt, and learn from one another in the process. Working together to create a literary quilt for a text along with reviewing other group's quilts enable students to construct and deconstruct meaning, helping to solidify student analysis of how literature comments on life (Schlick Noe and Johnson 1999).

At the beginning of the project, groups should spend time researching the history of quilt making. Different cultures throughout history have used quilts as narrative tools to record, life experiences and community events. For example, some historians believe that quilts were used in the Underground Railroad to communicate secret messages to enslaved individuals seeking freedom (National Park Service 2011). Another historical example of using quilts to convey messages was the AIDS Memorial Quilt, which began in 1987 as a gigantic quilt to memorialize those who had died from illnesses related to AIDS. Each square of the quilt was created by loved ones of a person who was lost to the AIDS epidemic (Bennington-Castro 2021). So, get students involved in researching more about the history of quilts. These examples can serve as inspiration for the Literary Quilt Project.

Quilts begin with a pattern, but to keep things simple in the initial stages of the project, students can begin by using individual squares to brainstorm ideas and to sketch out mock-ups before deciding on a particular quilt pattern to use for the final project. Similar to a one-pager, students should aim to build a visual map of analysis based on a central idea. They should construct a thesis statement to use as the center square of the quilt and then include textual evidence, symbols character traits, plot points, conflicts, settings, and so forth to communicate the central theme. Groups can use any means of their choosing to create the individual squares to represent their visual interpretation of the theme. For instance, a student might create a dark and stormy square that represents the kind of turmoil that occurs in *Wuthering Heights*. Another student might create a colorful and vibrant quilt, square that connects to the pursued hopes and dreams of the Roaring Twenties embodied by the characters in *The Great Gatsby*. By constructing the quilt squares, students can make symbolic connections that lead to thematic analysis.

To create their quilts, groups can use construction paper, fabric, poster board, Canva, or any other material of their choice. This project encourages creative freedom, so think about letting students express their analysis in a creative format that they choose—from drawings to paintings to photographs to digital designs to actual sewing—because students love the chance to be creative when they can (Schlick Noe and Johnson 1999).

In addition, teachers can extend the project by requiring additional written components such as square labels with textual evidence or a reflective essay at the end. These written components give students a chance to explain their projects and how they used elements such as colors, shapes, photos, graphics, text, and patterns to represent their literary analysis. Again, the activity enables students to make connections between the visual representation and the text in a manner that communicates literary interpretation and demonstrates effective communication. See Figure 1.2 for an example of the Literary Quilt Project.

Innovative Alternatives to the Traditional Essay   17

FIGURE 1.2 Literary Quilt Project example.

To help focus the ideas of a group's quilt project and to differentiate this project for all learners, consider creating quilt square templates for different types of evidence. For example, students can choose to focus on characterization, symbolism, key events, or literary devices to prove their thesis statements. Once they decide on the types of quilt squares they would like to create, they can use the templates to sketch out a plan for each square. Foster creativity and show students plenty of models to set the expectations for the assignment and help inspire new ideas.

Once groups complete their quilts, they can present their assembled quilts to the class, explaining how each square contributes to the central theme or thesis claim. Alternatively, groups can hang their quilts around the room for a gallery walk, and students can select a quilt to evaluate. Another option includes a class discussion about the different themes and analysis among groups. Consider asking students reflective questions such as these:

- Which quilt did you find the most interesting and why?
- How did seeing the other quilt projects affect your understanding of the theme and interpretation of the novel?
- What new ideas about the text did you discover by completing this project?

The Literary Quilt Project promotes critical and creative thought about themes in literature, collaboration with peers, and artistic expression. Consequently, it forms an engaging and unforgettable mode of analyzing a novel, one that students will remember because of its uniqueness as compared to traditional assignments.

THE POSITIVE RUBRIC

This section explores the idea of reimagining the traditional essay rubric from what a student does wrong to what a student does well. Although I always strive to highlight at least one positive aspect of a student's writing, so I decided to create a rubric that emphasizes constructive feedback, focusing on strengths rather than solely pointing out areas for improvement. That is when I created the positive essay rubric concept. This rubric focuses on recognizing student strengths and areas of growth with the goal of building student motivation, efficacy, and skills development. It is a completely different way of approaching writing assessment. Not only does positive reinforcement encourage students to reflect on their work, but it also aligns with research that shows positive feedback builds confidence and can lead to better academic success. There is a reason why a teacher saying "Good job" can go a long way—and research supports this concept. Let's look at what the research shows:

- According to Susan Brookhart's (2017) book *How to Give Effective Feedback to Your Students*, focusing on strengths and providing specific, constructive feedback leads to improved student performance.
- Hattie and Timperley's (2007) research suggests that constructive and positive feedback leads to best learning. When feedback focuses on students' strengths and gives them specific ways to work on areas of growth, they can become more motivated and more likely to take risks in exploring new writing approaches.
- Daniel M. Fienup (2019) shows that positive reinforcement, especially when accompanied by positive teaching methods, can significantly boost grades and lower disruptive behavior of students with combined behavioral and learning disabilities.

This research inspired me to create a positive essay rubric that functions much differently than a conventional essay rubric. Instead of only focusing on problems with student writing, this rubric points out the positives and then gives actionable revision steps to consider with the opportunity to earn points back based on revisions. By focusing on praise instead of criticism, students are more receptive to overall feedback. According to Carol Dweck (2006), when we give specific, "process-oriented feedback," we nurture a growth mindset (p. 206). This way of thinking leads students to consider difficulties as chances to grow and develop rather than as something that negatively affects self-esteem—Positive reinforcement opens students' willingness to absorb constructive criticism instead of shutting down.

To set up the positive rubric, award points based on a list of skills. For example, the rubric could have the following list of targeted writing skills for an introduction paragraph to a literary analysis essay:

Targeted Writing Skills	Positive Feedback 1 +20	Positive Feedback 2 +20	Recommended Revision
Attention-Grabber	Your attention-grabber immediately grabs the reader's attention in an effective way and establishes a captivating tone for the essay. It is engaging and makes me want to read more—great work!	You've started your essay with a creative and intriguing hook that sparks the reader's interest. It connects well to the topic of the thesis statement and leaves a strong first impression!	Earn up to 20 points by revising or adding an attention-grabber to hook the reader from the start. Try beginning with a surprising fact, a vivid description, or a quotation from the text.
Author's Full Name	Excellent work introducing the author's full name in your introduction and for spelling it correctly! This demonstrates your attention to detail and establishes your credibility as a writer.	Great job including the author's full name in the introduction. It shows that you understand the importance of giving credit to the writer from the start. Your reader will fully understand whose work the essay analyzes.	Earn up to 20 points by including the author's full name in your introduction to give proper credit for the text you are going to analyze. Double-check the spelling to ensure accuracy as this adds to your credibility as a writer.
Thesis Statement Claim	Your thesis statement is clear, focused, and narrowed to address the specific theme of the text. It provides a strong foundation for your essay and logically connects to the evidence.	Great job crafting a thesis that is both insightful and focused! Your claim is logical and stated as a narrowed theme statement, making it easy for the reader to understand your interpretation of the text.	Earn up to 20 points by revising your thesis to make it more focused and developed as a theme statement instead of just a thematic topic. Make sure the theme is not just a single word idea, and be sure it clearly reflects your interpretation of the text.

Targeted Writing Skills	Positive Feedback 1 +20	Positive Feedback 2 +20	Recommended Revision
Thesis Statement Evidence	Your thesis statement does an excellent job incorporating specific evidence in the form of literary elements and techniques that support your theme. It sets a clear road map for the body paragraphs.	Great work including precise and relevant evidence in your thesis statement! This strengthens your argument and provides a clear structure for how your body paragraphs will develop your ideas.	Earn up to 20 points by revising your thesis statement to include specific literary devices that directly support your theme. This will help prove your interpretation and provide a foundation for the analysis in your body paragraphs.
Transition Between Intro and Thesis	Your transition from the attention-grabber to the thesis statement is smooth and natural. It guides the reader into the thesis statement in a logical way.	Excellent job connecting your attention-grabber to your thesis statement! The flow is engaging, ensuring the reader stays interested in your overall argument.	Earn up to 20 points by revising the transition between your attention-grabber and thesis statement to gradually narrow the focus of your introduction. This will help guide the reader from the broad attention-grabber into the specific thesis statement.

As the sample rubric shows, a positive rubric works much differently than a classic rubric. To grade the introduction paragraph (in this example), I would select one of the two positive comments if the student executes the skill effectively. In this case, the student can earn 20 points for the skill that receives a positive comment. However, if a student needs further work on a specific skill, I require revisions for that skill and then conference with the student on their changes. At that point, I assign the student a final grade and commend them for their dedication in improving their writing. Although this method involves revision and resubmission, it works! It is an entirely different way to grade, but it builds student confidence in writing.

By assigning a final grade to an essay without any requirement to go back and make corrections, students merely keep repeating the same mistakes over and over again. I have seen students get frustrated with too many negative comments, shut down emotionally, and throw away their essays as they walk out of the classroom. That does not do any good for student growth or efficacy. By reshaping how we grade to focus on the positive and allowing for revisions that help students master important skills, we can get better writing results. We must think outside the confines of past pedagogy. We must put ourselves in the shoes of our students whose writing abilities have trended downwards as technology usage has trended upwards. The positive essay rubric focuses on the strengths within student work and encourages growth with constructive, supportive feedback.

The Innovative ELA Teacher Pack

Don't forget to access the Innovative ELA Teacher Pack of 50 FREE and EXCLUSIVE resources through the following QR code. Simply follow the QR code over to the Bespoke ELA website to download all 50 FREE resources that accompany the assignments, lessons, activities, and projects found in this book.

Scan the QR code.
Then use the password
JaneAusten1775
to log in and download.

CHAPTER TWO

Innovative Approaches to Editing and Revision

Along with innovative ways to assess writing skills, we can also integrate more innovative methods for editing and revising writing. There are three occasions in my classes when I tend to hear students grumble and complain:

- When they need to read
- When they need to write an essay
- When they need to edit and revise a piece of writing

But why does this happen? The reading and writing process demands a steady application of energy, stamina, and often the kind of patience that our students, can find difficult to muster because they are accustomed the instant gratification of today's tech world. The task of going back through a piece of writing to make it better can seem overwhelming, so as English teachers we see writers oftentimes turn in a rough draft as the final draft of an essay. We see students skip over editing and revising completely. We see them not really care about making their writing better. But why? It is boring, and it is hard. Yet, these are life skills as well as academic skills that students must master. The challenges we face to engage our students in the process of editing and revision necessitate change. How can we inspire them to take an active interest in refining their writing without giving up?

We can use best practices in the build of our lessons. Crafting learning experiences involves the same tenets of student engagement: collaboration, student choice, physical movement, and gamification. This does not mean we need to turn every lesson into a thrilling, tap dance performance. After all, that's not what students will experience in their careers—unless they become dancers. But we can use interactions such as peer review and teacher-student conferences, to make the mundane tasks of writing, revising, and editing more interesting. Steve Graham and Dolores Perin (2007) argue for the "process Writing Approach, which interweaves a number of writing instructional activities in a workshop environment that stresses extended writing opportunities, writing for authentic audiences, personalized instruction, and cycles of writing." By using approaches like these, we can see better engagement from our students in their writing. The strategies outlined next are intended to help students connect more with the writing process.

Around the World Revision: A Peer Editing and Revision Game

In this activity, students take a peer's essay and then visit editing and revision stations around the classroom that guide them through the process of giving meaningful feedback. This activity's physical movement helps to maintain student interest because it keeps students awake and energized rather than just sitting at a desk the entire time. It also enables learners to collaborate and help each other as a writing community. This concept echoes Robert Marzano's (2007) sentiments in his book *The Art and Science of Teaching: A Comprehensive Framework for Effective Instruction* where he explores ways to boost student performance and motivation through incorporating physical movement and gamification into the classroom. He argues that these techniques can significantly enhance student involvement in their work. And he's right—making an activity fun through friendly competition can spark students' positive feelings toward an assignment.

The Around the World Revision Game aims to create a friendly, competitive atmosphere wherein groups race against each other to revise and edit a piece of writing. By gamifying these necessary skills, the mundane process of editing and revision morphs into a fun, friendly competition that gets results. Here's how it works:

1. **Prepare for peer revision.** Teachers organize students into groups of three to four and assign all groups the same essay to revise and edit, providing each student with a copy that they can take around to each station. Clipboards come in handy here if you have them available. This essay needs to be a draft with plenty of errors for students to identify and correct. Even though each student has a copy of the essay, they should assign one person in their group to mark a master version of the essay that will be assessed for points in the game. That way, when a group comes to check their score, the teacher can assess only one copy for the group's score instead of several students' versions.

2. **Score points and win the game.** To score points, student groups must complete all station activities and then check their edited and revised draft with the teacher, who awards one point for each meaningful, correct, or effective change to the essay. The team with the most points at the end of the game, wins!

3. **Set up stations.** Here are some station ideas to use for the Around the World Revision Game

    - **Thesis tune-up.** At this station, the group focuses on the thesis statement and labels its key components—claim and evidence or reasons. Students also ensure that the argument uses a logical claim and outlines a clear road map for the essay

    - **Topic takeoff.** Here, students locate topic sentences and determine whether the sentences summarize the main ideas of each paragraph. They also check to see if the paragraphs flow nicely by starting with transitions and if the organization of ideas across the essay makes logical sense. Furthermore, they look for any thesis reminders in the topic sentences so that they can stay focused on the main argument.

- **Evidence express.** At this station, students check that each body paragraph contains two to three pieces of textual evidence to support the topic sentence. They should also ensure that each quotation is smoothly embedded within an original sentence, rather than left to stand alone. Quotations should be purposefully selected to prove the topic sentence. If a quote seems too long, the peer reviewer can make edits to shorten it as needed.

- **Commentary corner.** This is the most difficult part of the writing process because it requires analysis. Students should check to make sure that the writer has explained what each quotation shows and has not summarized or paraphrased the quote in lieu of analysis and explanation. They also need to make sure that the commentary fits the quotation and doesn't address something else not shown by the evidence.

- **Word wizards.** Here, students focus on editing the vocabulary used in the essay draft. They concentrate on the precision of word choice and remove any common language such as cliché expressions (e.g., "peaceful like a dove") or idiomatic sayings (e.g., "up the creek without a paddle"). Students should also circle any words that are not used correctly and replace basic words with higher-level vocabulary. In addition to that, they should check for any misused words such as *its* versus *it's* or *their* versus *there*.

- **Grammar gurus.** At this station, students edit the sample essay for grammar and mechanics. Instead of correcting every single grammar rule in the book, they can look for targeted grammar skills that they've been working on in class such as commas in compound sentences or subject-verb agreement. Students can, of course, correct all grammar errors they catch in an essay draft; however, a suggested list can help narrow the search for the editing and revision game.

- **Spelling sleuths.** At this station, students hunt for and circle words that are spelled incorrectly. This also includes any names of authors or names in citations that can sometimes be spelled incorrectly. Moreover, students can continue to look for incorrect versions of words such as *effect* versus *affect* and *here* versus *hear*.
- **MLA format factory.** At this station, students examine the essay for MLA format. They should check the essay's heading, page numbers, title, font, spacing, margins, and MLA citations. Again, if they find any errors with MLA format, they should correct them at this station.

These editing and revision stations offer a starting point and can shift depending on the targeted writing skills. Again, to win the game, each group should create a master draft that contains their edits and revisions. Groups can count their own points (one point per editing mark or revision) and then bring it up to the teacher for verification. Consider giving out prizes to groups such as highest score, best vocabulary revision, best quotation revisions, best grammar editing, and so on. Giving out prizes to winning groups will get them excited. I've found that students today will do just about anything for Takis and lollipops.

Editing and revising can be tedious, but by gamifying the process, it can become a bit more fun and more engaging. That's the goal of the Around the World Revision Game: combining gamification and movement to make revision far more engaging than working alone.

Grammar Guru Bingo

The Grammar Guru Bingo Game creates an enjoyable and memorable experience to practice identifying typical editing mistakes seen in student writing. I use this activity to support students' understanding of grammar concepts and rules by helping them find and fix common errors that pop up in their writing. After playing rounds of Grammar Guru Bingo, students can apply the grammar skills learned by playing the game to edit a piece of their own writing. Grammar Guru Bingo not only reinforces student understanding of common grammar mistakes but also provides practical examples of grammar issues to watch for in their own work. Integrating grammar instruction into engaging activities enables students to see grammar as a practical tool in effective communication rather than as a set of isolated rules that are difficult to remember (Dean 2008). Here are the basic steps for how to play Grammar Guru Bingo:

1. **Create bingo cards.** To start this game, first create bingo cards that contain sentences with common grammar errors in each bingo square. See Figure 2.1 for a sample Grammar Guru Bingo card. The

Editing and Revising
B I N G O

B	I	N	G	O
I love reading literature, it teaches us to explore different perspectives.	I can't wait to here the new book you read.	Before we go let's make sure we have everything we need.	The students worked on their essays in the library.	Each of the students must bring their own notebook to class.
The teacher assign too much homework every night.	I wanted to go to the store but it was closed.	She decided to hit the hay and get some rest.	I have a big test tomorrow; so, I need to study all night.	She tried to quickly finish her homework before dinner.
Running down the hall, the backpack slipped off Jake's shoulder.	Because I was late to school.		She enjoys reading, writing, and to paint.	She said, I'll meet you at the park".
Suddenly I realized I had left my keys at home.	Yesterday, she had went to the store to buy some groceries.	My favorite book is to kill a mockingbird by Harper Lee.	The cake was eaten by the children before the party even started.	When Sarah met Emily, she said she had a great idea for the project.
My brothers car is parked in the driveway.	My small fluffy dog loves to run, and play.	I love to read books I could spend all day in the library.	She is the one whom won the award.	I bought apples, oranges and bananas.

FIGURE 2.1 Example of a Grammar Guru Bingo card.

game moderator, who can either be the teacher or a student, uses cards that contain different types of grammar errors on them such as "comma error." When the moderator draws a card and calls out the grammar error, students search their bingo cards for a sentence that contains that error. Here are common grammar errors to consider including in the game (Hume Center for Writing and Speaking 2025):

- Subject-verb agreement error
- Dangling participle
- Sentence fragment error
- Pronoun-antecedent agreement error
- Misplaced modifier
- Split infinitive
- Semicolon error
- Parallel structure error
- Compound sentence comma error
- Run-on sentence error
- Complex sentence comma error
- Clichés or idioms
- Missing comma after an introductory element
- Quotation format error
- Commas in a series (Oxford comma) error
- Verb tense error
- Comma splice error
- Word use errors
- Then vs. than
- Affect vs. effect
- Its vs. it's
- There/ Their/ They're
- To/ two/ too
- Me vs. I
- Who vs. whom

- Who's vs. whose
- Who vs. that
- Your vs. you're
- Lay vs. lie
- Loose vs. lose
- Capitalization error
- Passive voice error
- Confusion between fewer and less
- Hyphen error
- Possessive noun error
- Misspelled words
- Vague pronoun error
- Unnecessary comma

Helpful Hint: Bingo can get messy with chips, coins, or pieces of paper to cover spaces. I'd recommend having them use a marker, highlighter, or pen to mark spaces. Students should also label the error in each sentence on the bingo card so that they can check their answers when someone scores a bingo. This also helps to build a resource to use for editing writing by giving students examples of commons error to avoid in their essays.

2. **Play the game.** To begin playing, first pass out bingo cards to each student. They can color in the free space in the center and prepare to listen to the different types of grammar errors called out by the moderator. As the moderator draws each card and calls out the type of grammar error (i.e., "subject-verb agreement error"), students look for an example of that error in one of the incorrect sentences on their bingo cards. If the student doesn't see it or recognize it, they do nothing and wait for the next grammar error to be called. If the student sees a sentence containing the error that was called out by the moderator, he or she should mark the space by

writing the name of the error (e.g., possessive pronoun error, pronoun-antecedent error, etc.) onto the bingo card space with the sentence that showcases the error.

3. **Win the game.** Similar to traditional bingo, when a student gets five in a row (up, down, or diagonal), they shout out, "Bingo!" The game moderator checks the student's card to make sure that the called errors are marked correctly on the student's bingo card. The winning student receives a prize—candy, chips, bonus points, a team badge, and so on. To keep playing the game, students can keep their same cards or swap cards. They can even create their own bingo cards by writing sentences that contain grammar errors.

Once students have played Grammar Guru Bingo, they can repurpose their bingo cards as editing guides to edit a piece of writing. Because the cards highlight common grammatical and spelling errors, they serve as a handy reference guide to use during writing workshop. Additionally, they can share their bingo cards with peers to understand errors they may have overlooked. This collaborative approach enhances peer revision and promotes a supportive learning environment and writing community in the classroom. As Vygotsky's (1978) theory of the zone of proximal development suggests, peer collaboration provides opportunities for students to learn from one another, bridging gaps in understanding and reinforcing skills through social interaction. Incorporating this teamwork aspect can bolster student writing skills in a supportive community of their peers. Thus, extending the bingo game into a collaborative peer revision activity helps to build student engagement in the writing workshop process.

Revision Relay Race

Students enjoy the Revision Relay Race because it helps them build stronger writing skills in another interactive, competitive format. In this activity, students take part in a relay race focused on editing and revising sentences. As stated previously, adding in friendly competition to any lesson boosts energy and excitement. Kagan (1994) supports the concept that employing cooperative learning structures, such as team-based games, heightens student participation, encourages collaboration, and drives active participation and ownership in the academic learning process. The Revision Relay Race does just that and can be implemented in several different ways to effectively support the development of writing skills. Here's one way to play the game that my students enjoy:

1. **Create teams.** Divide the class into teams of three to five students and give them an opportunity to select a team name. They have fun giving their teams an identity by creating a team name and perhaps a team logo or team flag. The more students can take time to develop their team identity, the more they buy into the gamification of academic content.

2. **Play the game.** To set up the relay, create a race folder for each team, which can be a simple file folder. Inside each folder, include the following items:

    - An essay rough draft (the same one for the entire class) with enough copies for each member of the group

    - Four editing tasks, each enclosed in a numbered envelope. See Figure 2.2 for photos of the Revision Relay Race folder. As a relay race, each member of the team takes a turn completing the revision task from their envelope. In this way, "passing the baton" means the next group member opens his or her envelope and then completes the revision task instructions. It's important to note that as a relay race, only one member of the team goes at a time while other group members cheer on their teammate. Teammates cannot write on the essay draft if it is not their turn, but they can answer questions or provide help if a team member struggles with his or her revision task. Resembling a real relay race, the first team to finish wins the game—but only if their revisions are correct and effective!

Innovative Approaches to Editing and Revision

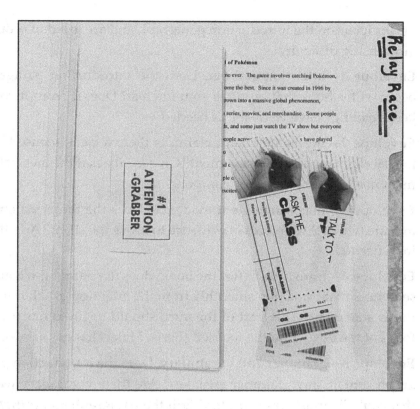

FIGURE 2.2 Revision Relay Race folder.

Helpful Hint: If a team has only three members, one student can go twice, and if there are five members, the fifth student can add any editing marks he or she chooses. The last person in a real relay race, the "fastest" team member or anchor, can take the final leg, so consider arranging the revision task envelopes from easiest to hardest to mirror the structure of a relay race and allow students the opportunity to decide on the order of their teammates.

Here are some suggestions for editing and revision tasks for the relay race envelopes. I would suggest focusing on a specific paragraph of an essay at a time so that students do not get overwhelmed with editing and revising an entire essay all at once. The following tasks focus on the introduction paragraph and are listed in order of increasing difficulty:

- **Envelope 1—attention-grabber.** Does the introduction paragraph begin with a hook that captures your interest? Does it prompt you to keep reading? Give feedback as needed.
- **Envelope 2—thesis statement claim.** Is there a clear, focused, and logical claim in the thesis statement? Give feedback if the thesis statement needs one of these key components.
- **Envelope 3—thesis statement evidence.** Does the thesis statement include two to three pieces of evidence to prove the claim? Add these in as needed.
- **Envelope 4—transition.** After the hook, does the paragraph contain sentences that transition smoothly from the attention-grabber to the thesis statement? This part of the intro should begin to narrow the focus of the essay into the focused thesis. Make changes as needed.
- **Envelope 5—grammar and vocabulary.** Does the introduction paragraph contain any grammar mistakes? Are there vocabulary words that could be more sophisticated? Edit the paragraph accordingly.

3. **Win the game.** A team wins a game round based on both speed and accuracy. As teams complete the relay race, the final team member brings his or her team's paper to the teacher, and the teacher numbers them in the order they finish (1st, 2nd, 3rd, etc.). The teacher can then quickly assess revisions and edits for accuracy, thoroughness, and impact to assess the winning groups. Finishing first doesn't guarantee a win if the group hasn't completed each step accurately. I consider both accuracy and speed to decide on the top three winning groups and give out prizes accordingly. Teachers can use their creativity to make unique awards or badges to award teams. After all, these serve as motivating factors to keep students engaged. To continue into another round, prepare another set of envelopes that focus on the next part of the essay like the first body paragraph or give students a new draft to revise and edit. Students can continue to race

through editing and revising the draft as time permits. A full essay draft could allow for at least four or five rounds:

1. **Round 1:** Introduction paragraph
2. **Round 2:** Body paragraph 1
3. **Round 3:** Body paragraph 2
4. **Round 4:** Conclusion paragraph
5. **Round 5:** MLA format

As with every activity in this book, teachers can adapt the Revision Relay Race to meet student needs. To modify this game, group members can work together on each revision task instead of tackling them individually. In this variation, students collaborate as a team to finish the tasks as quickly and correctly as possible. To accommodate a diverse range of learners, consider these other modifications:

- **Add in lifelines.** Remember the game *Who Wants to be a Millionaire?* Consider adding in lifelines, but instead of "phone a friend," the lifeline could be "talk to the teacher," which allows the group to call the teacher over for help on a specific revision task. Instead of "ask the audience," students could "ask the class" to receive help from anyone in the classroom—even a student from another group. Get creative with it and come up with even more lifelines. For this game variation, I include lifeline tickets in each group's game folder. Students give me their lifeline tickets as they use them.

- **Change the pacing.** Instead of having groups race to finish first, make the game more about accuracy. This way, groups can take as long as they need to complete the revision tasks and do not have to feel rushed. The time element can certainly cause anxiety, and we want to avoid this so that learners do not associate writing with negative feelings.

- **Differentiate roles.** Consider designating specific revision roles for each student in a group so that they can direct their attention to one task at a time and gain expertise in that area. Rather than having students randomly select an envelope with an unfamiliar task, allow them to choose a role that corresponds with their strengths. Some examples of more familiar roles include "word wizard," "grammar guru," and "textual evidence tracker." This approach promotes revising with purpose and promotes holding each group member accountable for a part of the essay revision.

In the end, the Relay Revision Race provides a high-energy and interactive way to transform the often-tedious work of revision into something fun. Although it seems like the perfect exercise to save for the last editing session, students can play this game at any time during the writing process. By incorporating elements of a relay race, this activity not only adds excitement to the often-monotonous task of editing and revising but also encourages teamwork, strategy, and collaboration.

The Wikipedia Errors Tour

For years, I wondered why my students seemed to forget grammar lessons so quickly. Even after completing multiple exercises on a specific skill, they still make the same mistakes in their writing. This made me realize that bridging the gap between learning and application is crucial. My experience has shown that we tend to remember moments that truly resonate with us emotionally. As Willingham (2009) explains, memory closely relates to meaning and emotion, and students are more likely to retain information when they engage in meaningful, interactive activities rather than mundane, repetitive drills. When we replace this type of learning with dynamic and interactive activities, students are not only more excited to participate but also more likely to recall proper grammar usage and apply it to real writing situations—for example, in letters, marketing content, social media posts, and the like. That is where this Wikipedia Errors Tour comes in!

As English teachers, we know that Wikipedia pages can be edited and revised by the public (with an approved account, of course), which makes Wikipedia an unreliable source for research (even though it's a great starting place to find credible sources). This open-source structure means that errors, such as confusing paragraphs or grammatical mistakes, can occasionally slip through to published pages on the website. Even Wikipedia's editing challenges, called Wikimanias, haven't completely eradicated these issues. That's why I created the Wikipedia Errors Tour Project—to provide students with a hands-on opportunity to identify and correct errors found on Wikipedia pages. According to Noa Aharony (2010), teaching students to critically evaluate and edit online content like Wikipedia not only improves their digital literacy skills but also reinforces critical thinking and attention to detail. Here is how this Taylor Swift–inspired activity works:

1. **Get started.** Divide the class into groups for the team challenge. Each group then searches for specific grammar or word-use errors in a Wikipedia entry. For instance, to practice identifying errors within complex sentences, students can search for, say, five examples of incorrectly punctuated complex sentences from any Wikipedia page of their choice. By allowing them to choose which Wikipedia pages to edit, they can select topics they are interested in, which also increases the interest factor of this activity.

2. **Find errors.** As students find errors, they can collect them and record them onto a Google Slideshow to share with the class. Typically, I like to have them look for three to five examples of each error. Because students can't necessarily edit Wikipedia pages, they can, instead, take screenshots of the errors they find and then place the image along with corrected sentences onto slides.

3. **Present errors.** Groups then present their findings to the class and explain how they corrected each error. Essentially, students take the class on a tour of the errors they found and corrected. Groups should explain the grammar rule that was broken in each example, give a revised version of the sentence, and explain what they did to correct the error.

4. **Write.** Following the presentations, have the students edit an essay draft for the same grammar skills. This targeted, hands-on approach should help reinforce newly acquired knowledge and encourage writing revisions at the level of syntax and sentence structure in student writing.

5. **Award badges.** I like to award badges to teams for this activity, themed after Taylor Swift, of course. Awarding badges and maintaining up-to-date team standings creates a friendly and fun rivalry in the classroom and helps to keep students consistently engaged throughout the year. Here are a few Swift-inspired badges to award for the Wikipedia Errors Tour Project:

- The "Style" badge for the group with the most stylish slideshow
- The "Ready for it?" badge for the group that was most prepared to present to the class
- The "Look What You Made me do" badge for the group that presented the most varied examples

Be imaginative and create badges that resonate with students. Use student interest inventories to discover what they like and then create awards based on what they like. This personalized approach not only boosts motivation but also transforms the Wikipedia Errors Tour into an exciting, student-centered celebration of critical thinking and attention to detail.

Word Salad Revision Game

This game focuses on increasing the sophistication of vocabulary in essay writing through a fun, interactive word activity. Adding this game into a writing workshop helps students increase the sophistication of their vocabulary. Essentially, students select an essay draft to revise for vocabulary and collect words in a "salad bowl." The salad bowl concept can be replaced with any other type of food that appeals to students such as bibimbap, pho, ramen, stew, pasta, pizza, and so on. The food type and dish serve a construct to use in the game as a placeholder for words, so any of these other food types work the same. According to Michael Graves's (2006) book *The Vocabulary Book: Learning and Instruction*, playful and creative approaches to vocabulary acquisition engage students in active learning, fostering deeper connections to new words and encouraging application in their writing. The following steps explain how to implement this fun vocabulary activity:

1. **Get started.** The goal of the game is for a team to collect as many high-level vocabulary words in the word salad bowl as possible, and the team with the most words, wins. To start, each student takes out an essay draft that they have been working on in class. Students then look through their own drafts and highlight (or circle) their most sophisticated (SAT-level) vocabulary words.

2. **Create the word salad.** Students then add their sophisticated words to the group word salad bowl. I've even brought in plastic bowls and had students write each sophisticated word on slips of paper we pretended were noodles, turning vocabulary practice into a playful bowl of word soup. It was super simple, but they had fun with it. Students should also check that each word going into the salad meets the SAT level of sophistication. When in doubt, students can check with the teacher to decide if a word stays or goes. Next, each group should add up how many words they have in their "salad bowls" and remove any duplicates. Feel free to give a reward to the group with the most words at this point. There will be other opportunities for groups to win in the next parts of the game.

3. **Add new words.** Now comes the fun part—the race to add sophisticated words to an essay draft. There are several ways to scaffold this part of the activity. Here are a few options to differentiate this part of the game:

    - **Option 1.** Give students a thesaurus to use for finding new, more sophisticated words in their essays.

- **Option 2.** Provide students with a curated list of specific vocabulary—especially vivid verbs—to guide their word choice and sharpen their writing. To take it a step further, challenge them to replace passive constructions with active voice for bonus points.
- **Option 3.** Give students an even shorter list of words or allow them to work together as a group to revise the vocabulary of the same essay instead of working on an individual piece of writing.

For any of these options, students can work as a team to increase vocabulary sophistication. Each student adds in as many new, sophisticated words to their draft as they can. They can work with their team members to help each other with new vocabulary words and to check revisions; however, each student should work on their own individual essay draft so that this game fits into writing workshop. To keep learners on track, give them a set amount of time (such as 20–30 minutes) to add new, higher-level words to their drafts. After this step, students then add any new word noodles to the bowl based on the words they added to their drafts.

Helpful Hint: Before each student officially adds a new word to an essay draft, have them check to make sure that the sentence uses the new word correctly. This helps to deter students from just stuffing words, or ingredients, into the "salad bowl" that don't make sense in context.

4. **Win the game.** When time's up, have groups tally their word noodles for a final score—prizes go to the team with the most! Wrap up the fun by awarding badges or small prizes to celebrate the winning groups.

To expand on this idea, create a collaborative salad swap challenge. by having (combine sentences) students swap their word salads with another group. Each group can then review the other's vocabulary words searching for words that they can add to their own essays. The Word Salas Revision Game not only encourages peer evaluation but also inspires creative thinking about how to enrich writing with fresh vocabulary.

Writing Makerspace

A writing makerspace provides a valuable resource to support students through the writing process. While there are many ways to house a makerspace in the classroom, I like to use a bulletin board as the makerspace station filled with handouts that focus on various writing skills. However, teachers can use something like a simple table or file folder crate to accomplish the same concept—or even house these resources online. The makerspace approach enables students to take what they need as they move through the writing process, and it is easier to differentiate instruction based on invidual skills. Additionally, creating a makerspace in the classroom enables learners to become more resourceful and independent with their own writing.

The bulletin board makerspace contains folders filled with minilessons and information about various writing skills. Research supports the effectiveness of the makerspace concept. According to Sciteach212 (2017) integrating a makerspace into the classroom promotes a learning environment centered on students and their experiences. It gives learners an opportunity to delve into content and sharpen their thinking and problem-solving skills. As Sciteach212 (2017) puts it, "In a maker environment, students literally construct their learning." Makerspace integration in classrooms increases student engagement and provides them with real-world skill-building opportunities. For example, a student struggling to craft a literary analysis thesis statement can check the makerspace for a guide on thesis development while another student who needs help with blending quotes can pick up a handout with the steps for how to do that—all from the makerspace. Other resources in the writing makerspace bulletin board might include tips on organizing paragraphs, adding transitions, adding depth to commentary, or avoiding common grammar mistakes. By offering a wide range of focused support materials, the makerspace enables students to take ownership of their editing and revision process, allowing them to select the help they need when they need it instead of sorting through an overwhelming number of resources online, some of which may

FIGURE 2.3 Writing makerspace in my classroom.

provide incorrect information. See Figure 2.3 for an example writing makerspace bulletin board. Some teachers opt to use QR codes instead of handouts, which can work effectively if students are allowed to use phones in the classroom. Our school does not, so we go with the handout method, and it works great.

Once I've pinpointed a specific pain point with a student's essay, I often direct the student to the makerspace for a resource that can help address that specific writing skill and require that they take the following steps before they conference with me: (1) read the resource from the makerspace, (2) attempt to apply the tips from the handout to editing and revising an essay, and (3) ask a classmate to clarify any confusion.

After these steps, the student can then conference with me to clarify any remaining confusion. Requiring students to take these steps before asking the teacher puts the responsibility on the student to seek out answers to their questions instead of expecting the teacher to do the work for them. How many times does a student ask us a question as a shortcut instead of searching for the answer on their own? The makerspace philosophy puts the tools at their fingertips and the onus on the student rather than on the teacher. After all, we hope to create independent, lifelong learners, and the makerspace bulletin board can facilitate that ownership of learning. If a student forgets how to do something, the student can go to the makerspace for a quick refresher on a skill.

The makerspace bulletin board can also house checklists or graphic organizers to help students navigate the writing process. For instance, in the brainstorming phase, writers can pick up a graphic organizer to help them get started with brainstorming methods. Additionally, when revising and editing, a student might pick up a checklist for self-editing or peer revision for a structured guide to improve an essay draft. The makerspace bulletin board can also feature resources for specific writing styles such as persuasive or personal narrative essays, giving students strategies curated to the type of assignment they are writing. As Nancie Atwell (2015) explains in her book *In the Middle: New Understandings About Writing, Reading, and Learning*, "Students need access to tools that help them draft, revise, and refine their work at their own pace, fostering independence and ownership over their writing process" (112). The makerspace gives them that access so that writers can get help any time they need it.

The Innovative ELA Teacher Pack

Don't forget to access the Innovative ELA Teacher Pack of 50 FREE and EXCLUSIVE resources through the following QR code. Simply follow the QR code over to the Bespoke ELA website to download all 50 FREE resources that accompany the assignments, lessons, activities, and projects found in this book.

Scan the QR code.
Then use the password
JaneAusten1775
to log in and download.

CHAPTER THREE

Innovative Writing Activities for the Real World

Even in the innovative classroom, traditional essays absolutely have their necessary place as part of English Language Arts (ELA) instruction. Every person needs to be able to write clear sentences, paragraphs, and arguments and be able to read texts for key ideas and data points just to live life as an adult. However, we can still find to engage students in the writing process by giving them more authentic, real-world writing experiences.

Real-world writing experiences tend to engage students more in the writing process for several reasons. First, real-world writing appeals to students' personal lives and interests. Traditional prompts such as the old standard school uniform persuasive essay come across as being disconnected from student interests. Kelly Gallagher (2011) points out that "students are more likely to engage in writing when they see a purpose beyond the classroom walls, a reason to communicate with an authentic audience" (48). When students can have an authentic audience for their work, they can see how writing can have an impact on society—and even change the world. That in itself can hook reluctant readers and writers. This chapter explores innovative writing assignments with real-world audiences to engage students in the writing process.

Classroom Blogs or Newsletters

I enjoy writing new blog posts for `BespokeClassroom.com`. Blogging gives me a creative avenue to explore ideas and share them with real-life English teachers, which makes the writing process more meaningful. We can use blogging or newsletters to give our students a genuine writing experience in the classroom. They can use a blogging platform to reach a real-world audience in the form of a class blog or newsletter that goes out to their classmates, school, teachers, administration, and/or parents. According to John McCarthy (2023), "Knowing their writing has an audience besides their teacher helps motivate students to do their very best work." Structuring writing workshop on a real-world publication comes with the added benefit of teaching important business skills such as organizing a group, delegating tasks, meeting deadlines, communicating problems and solutions, writing content that appeals to a targeted audience, marketing content, and much more. These publications are also a great way to get the whole school involved as well as the community because it takes the writing beyond the confines of the classroom walls. The comprehensive learning experience from real-world writing goes beyond traditional writing assignments in ELA that can seem superficial and unrelatable to students.

Tips for Implementing a Blog or Newsletter in Your ELA Classes

1. **Get started.** Start small. It's important to lay a solid foundation for a class publication before scaling it up to a larger audience or more frequent publication. Certain components need to be in place before the launch of the first blog or newsletter. The class needs to get organized by assigning roles, brainstorming ideas for content and sections, and creating a writing workshop process that writers can follow from draft to publication. The newsletter or blog can and will change over the course of a school year as students adjust the outcomes of each publication. Give plenty of time for them to reflect on feedback from the first publication before launching into the second one. As they become more confident with the process and

the product, students can gradually increase the frequency to a monthly or bimonthly publication.

2. **Assign roles.** Engage students with roles. Assigning roles, or having them apply for roles, gives each student a purpose and ownership of the class blog team, which can help with student accountability. I also like for students to rotate through different roles throughout the school year. To do that, I use job groups that rotate through the different roles in a set pattern. Here are a few job groups to consider using with student groups:

    - Editor team
    - Graphic design team
    - Marketing team
    - Creative team
    - Research team

    As students rotate through the different job groups, they work on different skills and tasks each time, resulting in practicing with an entire array of business and communication skills. To implement group expectations, I give each group a folder with their responsibilities and tasks. As student groups work through their specific tasks and assignments, the teacher acts as the editor-in-chief to help teams stay on task, answer questions, and provide guidance as needed.

    Helpful Hint: Before job groups rotate to the next rotation, consider having a mentor day in which groups train the new, upcoming group. This enables students to share their expertise about what they've learned from the role they've just completed. They can share tips and advice on how to best be effective in the new role.

3. **Use technology.** The technology aspect of creating a blog or newsletter can be daunting but start by using free blogging platforms and newsletter templates such as WordPress, Blogger, or Canva.

Another free platform, Google Sites, enables anyone to create a clean, simple website. Google Sites also allows for more control over what the website looks like and who can view or edit the content. Additionally, lots of schools have subscriptions to programs such as Adobe Express, which offer similar options as the free programs. Check with the technology specialist or curriculum coach at your school to ask about the tech options. Many of these resources also have high-quality templates, which let students focus on the content rather than the layout. Admittedly, we do not teach marketing in ELA, so we want our students to focus on the content more so than the user interface or design; however, learning the basic principles of marketing and design can give learners another skill set to take with them into their real-world careers. See Figure 3.1 for an example class newsletter made with a Canva template.

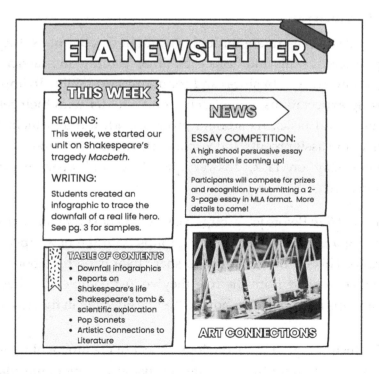

FIGURE 3.1 Sample class newsletter.

4. **Create content.** There are lots of ways to go about assessing student work through a collaborative project like this one. Every student in the class, no matter their roles in the publication process, should make written contributions to the publication in addition to their duties. This enables teachers to assess targeted writing skills once students complete a publication. The teacher can begin by giving directed assignments and then over time allow students to take more control over the content and publication process. Consider beginning with the personal narrative in the first publication and then moving on to other topics that interest students. Use backward design to plan out scaffolded writing skills to assess in each publication. Then, map out the remaining topical options for future publications so that each writing skill builds on the others in a logical manner.

   Helpful Hint: Consider partnering with other subject areas to include different types of writing in the publication that cross the content divide. For example, students can incorporate written tasks from other classes such as science experiments, history project reports, or geography infographics. Opening up the project to multiple disciplines gives students a chance to tap into their strengths in addition to ELA and helps them understand that all content areas involve writing, not just ELA.

5. **Use the writing process.** Incorporate the writing process into the class publication. Have students complete peer revisions of their work before submitting their contributions to the editor team, who then conferences with each student to finalize his or her work. This process encourages thoughtful revision and helps students improve their writing skills with purpose. Research shows that taking part in peer feedback not only enhances the quality of writing but also cultivates two essential 21st-century skills: critical thinking and collaboration (Graham et al. 2013). This project

encourages collaboration in-person and online, synchronously and asynchronously, remotely and in the classroom; thus, it gives students a snapshot of what it's like to work on a real business team in today's business world.

6. **Share the publication.** Market the class publication to a real-world audience. Students can invite their parents and families to read the newsletter or blog. Inviting guest contributors, from teachers to administrators to community leaders, establishes another way to connect with a real-world audience. Students may be more motivated and engaged in the writing process if they know others in the school and community are going to read their work. Consider a post-publication assignment to reflect on the publication and provide feedback on publications from other classes. Oftentimes, schools rate teacher performance partially on how a teacher involves the school community in their classes. This assignment clearly meets that goal.

7. **Celebrate the publication.** Celebrate each publication and share in the class's success. Use social media or email blasts to distribute publications with the public. Public recognition can build student pride in their work and encourage students to continue improving their writing.

Creating a class blog or newsletter where students can publish their writing for a real-world audience offers a more meaningful and authentic writing experience; thus, it prepares them for success in both college and beyond. Research indicates that writing for actual audiences increases learner commitment and helps them understand the significance of writing skills in their lives and future careers (McCarthy 2023). Morphing the ELA class into a journalism team that publishes content by students can get them excited about their writing journeys.

Advocacy Campaigns

At their core, advocacy campaigns are organized efforts with the goal of shedding light on a specific cause or issue. Allowing students to create advocacy campaigns on issues they are passionate about lets us harness the power of student choice along with an authentic audience. Research shows that when students get to engage in project-based learning that lines up with their interests, such as advocacy projects, they become much more motivated and develop a much deeper understanding of the content (Larmer et al. 2015). Let's look at how advocacy campaigns can ignite student passion and interest in ELA.

For this assignment, students develop and implement an advocacy campaign on a topic of their choice. I like to have groups create a social media account to house their campaigns, which enables students to interact with an authentic audience. As an important side note, before embarking on any project that deals with social media, please secure permissions from all necessary parties and consider keeping the accounts on private (if needed) to allow only fellow classmates to view and comment on the information. Alternatively, students can create a mock campaign using Canva to submit for a grade and then make it public if they so choose, perhaps for bonus points. To connect advocacy campaigns to essential ELA skills, consider including requirements like these:

- A persuasive thesis statement in the bio line
- A specially designed logo and name for the advocacy campaign that catches attention
- Three informative posts that share data and statistics from credible sources about the issue; students can cite sources in the comments.
- Two- to three-minute persuasive reels that deliver the heart of the group's persuasive message about their issue and campaign

- A unique hashtag that relates to the advocacy campaign that can be used on social media platforms
- Three posts of eye-catching images, graphics, and/or quotes to capture attention and convey the campaign message
- A repost from another account that fits the purpose and message of the advocacy campaign; students should be sure to ask for permission to repost and then give attribution for that shared post.
- Two posts of behind-the-scenes content to show the group's work to raise awareness for their cause
- Relevant and thoughtful group comments on each post to show interaction with the content
- An honest attempt to gain 100 authentic followers to connect with other people interested in the same cause

After students finish creating their social media advocacy campaigns, I grade their work by going through each social media account to assess skills such as thesis statement, persuasive techniques, organization, credible evidence, and following directions. Students can also assess other Advocacy Campaign Projects from their peers.

Helpful Hint: Consider giving bonus points to students who leave thoughtful comments on other groups' posts. Likewise, be flexible and open to recognizing student campaign milestones, such as making the news or going viral.

The Advocacy Campaigns Project enables students to voice their opinions on matters that they care about. It creates agency by showing how words can affect real, positive change in the world. Creating campaigns for the real world naturally makes the learning process more meaningful, transitioning students from passive learners into proactive, educated campaigners who are equipped to tackle issues that affect our world.

Business Proposals

A business proposal essentially presents a business concept—usually to an investor, a subject matter expert, or employees. The business pitch exists to convince potential investors, customers, or other partners to support the new business venture or invest money in the new project. Inspired by the TV show *Shark Tank*, in which new businesses pitch their ideas to a panel of investors, we can reproduce a similar concept in our classrooms. This gives students another innovative way to use real-life ELA skills that might even turn into a real-life business for a student at some point. I say that because I've had a student take the seed idea from this project and start his own vending machine business as a senior in high school. It was incredibly impressive, and it all started with the Business Proposal Project.

At the core, a good business idea solves a problem. It provides a product or service to make people's lives easier. Thus, students should start the project by brainstorming problems and then thinking of ways to solve them through the creation of a new product or service. They should also conduct research to make sure there's a need for the new product or service. Although the project does not require that students manufacture a product, they can, instead, create marketing materials, drawings, mockups, or 3D prototypes of their proposed product or service to use during their pitches. Finally, students pitch their new business concepts to the class who acts as a team of investors like those on the TV show. Investors can ask questions and give feedback to groups about their new business ideas and then vote on whether they want to invest.

But what makes a business pitch effective and successful? Here are the basic components:

- **Executive summary.** This concise, summative thesis statement presents the business concept and addresses the problem it solves.
- **Market analysis.** This component involves research into the specific market that the product or service falls into. It includes doing a competitive audit in which groups analyze the competition from similar

products or services to see how their idea compares to what already exists. For instance, if a group wants to design a new water bottle, they must first research existing bottle companies to see if there is a need for a new one.

- **Product/service description.** The group then presents a logical and persuasive description of the proposed product or service. Students explain how the business concept works, give a demonstration, or show mock-up drawings or sketches so that the investors can fully understand how the new business will function.
- **Business model.** Here, the group describes how the business venture will generate money and turn a profit. Students can explore how they will market and sell their product or service to the public by defining the specific audience for their business.
- **Financial projections.** Next, students can research the basic cost to create their product or service and then compute how much to charge for it. They can use this data to configure basic cost and profit projections.
- **Funding proposal.** Students then present a funding proposal that offers a clear statement of the group's financial needs from the investors and includes a detailed explanation of how the investors' money will be spent to further develop the business.

Helpful Hint: Consider devoting time to watching a few episodes of *Shark Tank*, which inspired this activity. Students can make notes on how individuals pitch their businesses and some of the rhetorical techniques they use to be convincing. They can also take note of the types of questions that the investors ask and then use those questions during the group business pitches.

Here are more specific details on the steps to follow to implement this project:

1. **Identify a problem and understand the audience.** Learners choose a real-life problem or inconvenience that they feel needs to be

resolved. Then, they then brainstorm products or services that can help solve the identified problem. The solution should be realistic and different from what other businesses have to offer, which means students need to conduct initial research. This initial stage focuses on investigating and understanding the needs of the intended audience. Understanding audience is a crucial aspect of the rhetorical situation, and students must have a thorough understanding of their customer so that they can best design a business that meets the needs of this audience.

2. **Develop business plan and conduct research.** At this stage, students conduct market research to see what other similar competition may exist. Known as a "competitive audit" in the business world, this essential step helps entrepreneurs fully understand their competition. If many companies are already working on a specific problem, a team must either pivot to another solution or go back to the drawing board to select another problem to solve with a different product.

3. **Analyze finances.** This part of the project presents a unique opportunity to work with teachers from other content areas such as math or economics. Students can conduct basic financial forecasting to decide how much it would cost to get their business started and how much money they could potentially make. In fact, other teachers may love to get involved and teach their classes about different finance strategies while students develop their product pitches in their ELA classes. Finally, groups should think about how best to market their product or service to consumers, which requires more research into the characteristics of the targeted customer.

4. **Prepare the pitch and pitch the idea.** Student groups create a five- to seven-minute business pitch in which they tell the class of investors about their product or service in a persuasive manner. Visual aids such as slides or videos can enhance the overall persuasion of the pitch. Students should also focus on integrating rhetorical

devices such as appeals to *ethos*, *pathos*, and *logos* to convince the investors to invest. Students can also write a persuasive pitch essay that summarizes their business idea, market research, and how their product or service solves a real-world problem.

5. **Vote on the business ideas.** After each presentation, the group engages with the class to answer questions and defend their business concept. Then, each member of the class votes on whether to fund a group's project or not. Students can vote by raising signs—green for go or red for no. However, there are other ways they can cast their votes, such as using polls on learning platforms such as Google Classroom or Canvas. Alternatively, students can cast their votes using Kahoot, Quizizz, or other creative methods—like drawing emojis to express approval or disapproval. Groups that win over most investors can win a prize, a new badge, candy, or other reward.

6. **Reflect on the experience.** As groups present, class members can rate each group's pitch and offer constructive feedback. After presentations have ended, students can reflect on the project Proposals in a few different ways:

   - Seek feedback from a real-life businessperson
   - Assign a grade to their own project, supported by evidence from their presentations
   - Hold a whole-class discussion about what they learned from the project and why persuasive communication matters in the real world

The Business Proposals Project enables students to practice essential ELA skills alongside experiencing what it's like to be an entrepreneur; it gives them a glimpse of what it's like to solve a real-world problem and build a business. Students love this activity and get so excited about being an innovator and creating something that matters to real people. As Tony Wagner (2012) argues in *Creating Innovators*, "When students are given opportunities to explore their passions and work on meaningful projects, they develop the skills and mindsets necessary to succeed in the real world" (123). The research shows that we need to make learning experiences more applicable to real life because it gives relevance to the learning process, which in turn builds the enigma of student motivation.

Movie Pitches

Screenwriting involves crafting scripts for film or television—powerful storytelling formats that shape much of our daily entertainment. Yet despite their cultural impact, they're rarely integrated into secondary ELA classrooms. Reading dramas, and sometimes performing them, presents the closest we come to this kind of writing in ELA. But why? Screenwriting, also called scriptwriting or screenplay writing, represents a genre that we should employ more frequently in secondary ELA because it has so much potential to engage students in learning. Who doesn't love a movie? But have you ever read a screenplay? Unless you're a screenwriter, then the answer is most likely no. Examining a movie script and contemplating how words become a film is an eye-opening experience in and of itself. As educators, we can home in on the framework of screenwriting and script analysis to elevate our students' skills (Dobbs 2017b).

Before we dive into the specifics of how this project works, it's important to understand how we can integrate the study of screenwriting into ELA curriculum. In crafting an original screenplay idea, students should first examine how core literary elements such as character, plot, setting, conflict, dialogue, and style work together to create overall thematic meaning. Students must also apply prior knowledge of narrative structure to create a believable storyline with believable characters. In this way, the Movie Pitch Project requires students to apply and synthesize their prior knowledge in a new format. Rather than analyzing popular literary characters, students analyze the characters they construct to make sure their interactions make sense for the plot and accurately convey the theme of the film. In essence, students showcase their understanding of literary elements and techniques through the process of constructing writing instead of analyzing, or taking apart, someone else's writing (Dobbs 2017b).

Here's how the Movie Pitch Project works:

1. **Get started.** For this project, students work with a group to create an original screenplay concept and then pitch their movie idea to the class. First off, students need to get into groups and learn the specific tools screenplay writers use to write their stories and bring them to life on the screen. These include learning new terms such as *plot treatment* and *subtext* as well as becoming familiar with screenplay format.

2. **Learn about screenplay format.** Ask students to read through screenplays of their favorite movies. Students can use these as models to learn about screenplay format and explore examples of subtext. Most screenplays can be found for free online through websites such as `SimplyScripts.com`. Furthermore, there are several YouTube videos about screenplay format and screenplay writing that we can use to teach students about the overall screenwriting and filmmaking processes. I like to give my students a few pages of the script for a popular movie to close read just like they would any other work of fiction. However, I also have them annotate the script for the format and have them pay particular attention to what each line of dialogue implies. Then, I show the same scene from the movie and have students make observations about how the script translates to the screen. Students typically find this experience eye-opening, and it helps them appreciate how movies are made.

3. **Brainstorm an original concept.** After students have a basic understanding of screenplay format, they can move on to brainstorming the plot and inventing characters for their own original screenplay concepts. Of course, the debate between Aristotle and Shakespeare

enters the conversation at this point—which matters more: the plot or the characters? Although there isn't a correct answer to this question, the creative writing process moves in the same recursive way that writing any other content does. Students may start with either characters or plot, but they undoubtedly end up going back-and-forth between the two as they develop an original story. Here are a few brainstorming exercises to help students generate a unique plotline (Dobbs 2023b):

- Invent a pair of star-crossed lovers—two people who should not be together because of their circumstances.
- Create a plot in which a person goes from rags to riches and learns a valuable life lesson along the way.
- Situate the story in a natural disaster that the main character must try and survive.
- Create a secret that needs to be uncovered, but something or someone stands in the way.

There are ample prompts online to take students through the brainstorming process. As with other projects, students should also research old movies to see if their movie idea has already been made into a film. Students can brainstorm several ideas and then pick their best one to take through the rest of the project.

4. **Write a plot treatment.** After that, students craft a plot treatment, a written summary of the film's plot. The treatment serves as an overview of the film and assists the writers in identifying places where the story might need some adjustment. However, the plot treatment goes beyond plot to include a description of the main characters, the title, and the logline (Dobbs 2017b).

Helpful Hint: A logline is a one-sentence (or short) "elevator pitch" of a film's concept. The logline serves as a tool for pitching movie ideas to producers. It needs to grab attention and convey the main plot and meaning of the film in a succinct format—long enough to share on an elevator ride. For instance, the logline for *Jurassic Park* could be "A group of visiting scientists must survive a dinosaur attack when the theme park's security system fails."

5. **Write the character sketch.** Along with the plot treatment, students also write a character sketch of the protagonist in their film, going more in-depth with the character's physiology, sociology, and psychology. Both the plot treatment and the character sketch allow for assessing writing skills such as MLA format, grammar, organization of ideas, and supporting details. As an extension to this part of the process, students can also write a character sketch of the villain as it pertains to their story, considering the villain's origin story and impact on the plot.

6. **Write the screenplay segment.** Although we do not have time in class to write a full-length screenplay (approximately 120–150 pages in length), students can, instead, write the first 10 pages of the screenplay (one page of a screenplay equals about one minute of screentime), considering how they can build exposition and incite action within the first 10 minutes of the movie.

7. **Create the trailer.** After students complete the written components, they move into creating the final part of the project: the movie trailer. Students should view multiple movie trailers to understand the basic components, purpose, and structure of trailers. They can then channel those insights into crafting their own engaging and persuasive trailers.

8. **Host the film festival.** Then comes the fun part! We have an in-class film festival in which students show their trailers to the class who act as potential producers looking to invest in a new movie idea. Each group shows their movie trailer and then presents their film concept to the class. After each group finishes, the producers (a.k.a. students) vote either to purchase or pass on the concept. Similar to previous activities, they can hold up signs or use a Google Form to vote on

awards for the movie ideas. These awards can include "Best Original Concept," "Most Interesting Protagonist," "Best Overall Trailer," "Most Evil Villain," and so on. Create awards that will resonate with your students and invite them to come up with their own award names. We've had the "G.O.A.T." award, the "It's Giving" award, and the "Slay Fire" award. My students also love to put on a pretend class awards ceremony in which I hand out certificates or trophies to make it more fun and engaging.

Helpful Hint: Consider assigning students to a specific genre that coincides with a theme or literary unit of study. For example, a teacher might require that students focus their movie concepts on epic hero journeys during a unit on *The Odyssey*. This strategy enables learners to showcase key genre concepts, such as the traits of the epic hero and heroic journey.

My students always love this project. They enjoy the challenge of creating something new and working together to create something that reflects their interests and understanding. This project also offers an effective technique to synthesize learning and works with any literary unit.

Investigative Journalism: The School Scoop

There are many definitions of investigative journalism, but they all come down to the same end goal: to uncover a truth. In this project, students act as investigative journalists to uncover a story about their school—from discovering how a teacher preps for classes to uncovering the source of cafeteria food. And as students do that, they need to remember two points: (1) the important role journalists play in maintaining accountability and (2) the power of investigative journalism to make positive changes in the world.

1. **Find a school issue.** To start off, students should brainstorm problems, issues, mysteries, and questions about the goings-on at school.

Alternatively, so as not to upset administration, teachers can provide students with an approved list of issues to investigate. Some common topics that students tend to investigate include school lunch, hallway traffic, student parking, phone usage homework and tests, bullying, student mental health, safety, discipline, educational technology, extracurricular activities, clubs and organizations, and curriculum. After selecting a topic, students should narrow the topic to something specific and focused as with all research projects. For example, for the topic of hallway traffic, students might narrow the focus to the hallway outside of the cafeteria at lunch time.

2. **Research the issue.** During the research and planning stage, students do the following:

   - Develop a specific research question to guide the investigation.
   - Create a detailed investigation plan.
   - Identify and interview potential information sources (e.g., students, teachers, administrators, parents, etc.).
   - Research public documents, records, and/or media coverage.
   - Conduct surveys and polls.
   - Assess sources for reliability and potential bias.

3. **Create an investigative report.** After the research and planning stage, students compile their findings into an investigative report to share with the class. The report should follow a similar structure to a persuasive essay. Having students create an investigative report about an issue that directly affects their daily lives can be more engaging than the traditional, persuasive essay. Again, it has a real-world connection that helps students see that their writing really matters.

   Helpful Hint: As a side note, this project can be embedded into a class blog or newsletter. Students can publish their investigative reports and see how their writing can make a real impact at school.

To begin the writing process, students can analyze investigative reports from leading news agencies to use as models for generating their own compositions. Such models give students an understanding of how to format an investigative report, including these necessary components:

- An attention-grabbing headline.
- A lead paragraph that introduces the issue and hooks the reader.
- Credible evidence that includes interviews, surveys, polls, and/or research.
- Analysis of the issue and presentation of possible solutions to solve or lessen the problem.

Throughout this process, students learn about creative nonfiction and how to use storytelling as a persuasive tool while also integrating facts from credible sources. Students should consciously include rhetorical devices and appeals to *ethos*, *pathos*, and *logos* to present their findings in a persuasive way. In essence, this project acts similar to a persuasive essay; though, by packaging it in the high-interest format of an investigation, students might show more interest in creating a high-quality product. However, while the persuasive essay focuses more on the end goal of persuading an audience to believe something or take an action, the end goal of investigative report aims to bring something unknown to light. Even so, the persuasive format of an investigative report can give teachers an opportunity to target rhetorical skills through the context of this project.

After completing the investigative news report, students have the option to take the project to the next level by creating an investigative news segment. In this stage students play the roles of reporter and news production staff while gaining hands-on experience in multimedia production—that is, taking their written work and packaging it into a lively multimedia presentation or recorded video news segment. By transitioning from written to visual and auditory media, students can develop their communication skills and, at the same time, learn how to adapt messages across platforms. Although this project crosses over into journalism, many students claim that they learn how to communicate in their journalism classes. The immediacy of a real-world audience with a focus on impactful interests creates the foundation for student engagement. Suzie Boss (2016) says, "Journalism gives students a tool to engage constructively and productively with what's going on in their lives." Applying these same principles to ELA gives us the same buy-in that journalism teachers see in their classes.

To produce the multimedia presentation or recorded news segment, students should analyze and include elements such as video montages, interviews, reporter commentary, music, and other elements to highlight the key subject at the center of the investigation. These components not only enhance the storytelling behind the issue but also serve to captivate the audience, making the message more impactful. Ultimately, this project extension into multimedia not only encourages collaborative participation but also enables students to practice a broad range of skills that can serve them later in their careers.

Helpful Hint: Select what works best for students—the written article, the multimedia presentation or news segment, or both. Students can also turn their investigation into a podcast episode if they prefer to present their investigation in this popular audio format instead. There are lots of free resources online that students can use to record and edit audio.

The Investigative Journalism Project offers English teachers a rich method to inspire student motivation by making the curriculum relevant to their lives. By making the learning matter to students, we can create an environment wherein students understand the relevance of their education and thus become more motivated toward their own academic studies. As noted by the National Council of Teachers of English (NCTE; 2022), "All learners need to be able to express themselves using writing, speaking, and visual representation using varied modes, genres, and platforms of communication. These competencies are essential to work, life, and citizenship, impacting who has access to conversations, who can speak, and who is heard."

Literary Vacation Itinerary

The Literary Vacation Itinerary Project stands out as one of my favorites because it incorporates the love of travel and engages students in a creative and practical way. For this project, students create a detailed vacation itinerary based on a literary work and/or author's life that requires them to apply research, budgeting, and planning skills to create a fun, educational vacation. This project not only fortifies crucial ELA skills—such as research, organization, and effective communication—but also familiarizes students with the often-overlooked task of budgeting. Schools today rarely teach this skill, yet it's one that everyone needs to learn. In the process of exploring the financial and logistical aspects of travel planning, students can develop a new respect for how much planning and money goes into taking a vacation. Here's how it works:

1. **Get started.** This project begins with the novel selection. This can either be teacher-selected or student-selected. However, a novel with a strong sense of place or setting usually works best so that students can plan vacation activities in specific locations. For example, *The Great Gatsby* clearly connects to three places: Chicago, New York City, and Long Island. Alternatively, students can focus on an author's life instead of a novel. In this case, students can use any author to inspire the itinerary details. For genres such as fantasy and science fiction, students may need to think more creatively about how to provide relevant experiences. For example, a vacation inspired by Ray Bradbury's novel *Fahrenheit 451* may include a tour of book shops, a visit to a firefighter museum, and a stop at Bradbury's hometown in Waukegan, Illinois.

2. **Make observations.** Because most students will not have experience with putting together a vacation itinerary, it's key that they take time to critically review existing examples to understand the components that go into creating one. They can then apply those same components to the creation of their own itineraries. These components typically include destinations, travel dates, trip

duration, transportation, accommodations, daily itineraries, activities and excursions, must-see sights, estimated costs, passport or visa requirements, and top recommendations for dining and lodging, among other details.

3. **Research ideas.** Once students understand how to organize a vacation itinerary and what to include, they should then collect a list of the key locations featured in the novel (real or fictional) or important locations from the author's life and then research actual travel destinations that match these settings. A vacation itinerary inspired by *The Great Gatsby* might include activities such as having teatime at The Plaza Hotel, exploring the shops on Fifth Avenue, a tour of Princeton University where Fitzgerald attended, or a day trip to the Hamptons to explore the kind of mansion the character might have called home. Every part of the trip should clearly connect to the novel and/or author's life.

4. **Create the itinerary.** After researching, students then plan out the day-by-day activities for a vacation that lasts about 5–10 days. Each daily itinerary needs to be specific and include details such as transportation, food, museum entry times, ticket costs, and so on. The itinerary should also include the specific details to guide tourists from morning to night. While building the itinerary, students should also think carefully about the organization of the vacation. For instance, it wouldn't make sense to go back-and-forth between Manhattan and Long Island multiple times; it would make more sense to see and do everything in one location before moving on to the next one.

Helpful Hint: I like to keep old travel books in my classroom for this project so that students can use them as a resource. They don't work for every novel, but students have been able to get lots of great tips from them when creating an itinerary for a classic novel. To gather even more resources, ask students or parents to donate their old travel guides or look for them at garage sales and thrift stores.

5. **Create an expense report.** To target financial literacy, students can create an Excel Spreadsheet that breaks down the costs of the entire trip. They can conduct research to determine the total cost of the vacation by taking into consideration expenditures such as flights, train tickets, rental cars, daily meals and activities, souvenirs, museum ticket costs, and other expenses.

   Helpful Hint: To make the financial literacy part of the project even more comprehensive and analytical, students could create different versions of their itinerary for different budgets. For example, they could create a luxury package as well as a budget package. Alternatively, consider giving students a fictional budget to work with for a family of four and let them modify their itineraries to stay on budget. For example, a family of four might be restricted to a budget of $5,000. Students can use this budget to make decisions about their vacation itineraries.

6. **Present the itinerary.** After creating the itinerary, students can present their itineraries in different ways. These strategies can include creating a travel brochure, website, multimedia presentation, or podcast episode. See Figure 3.2 for a sample of a student travel brochure inspired by *The Great Gatsby*. I prefer to have students present their itineraries in website form using a Canva template and include links to the places and experiences included on the trip. Then, students can review their peers' websites to vote for the vacation itinerary they liked the most. To account for how the vacation itinerary connects to the novel, students can either include a written reflection that explains the connections using textual evidence or share their connections in their presentations.

7. **Reflect on the project.** Students should then reflect on how creating the vacation itinerary deepened their understanding of the novel's setting and themes. They can also think about how the project helped them connect more with the novel. These reflections add significance to the project, making it more meaningful, impactful, and realistic.

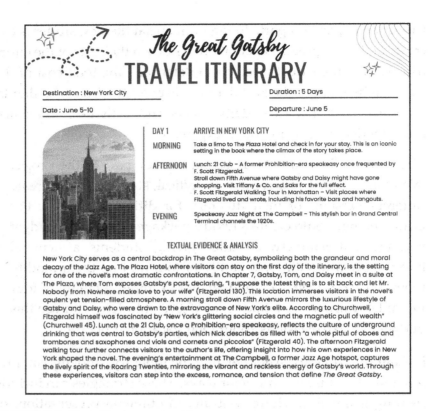

FIGURE 3.2 *Great Gatsby* vacation itinerary.

To summarize, the Literary Vacation Itinerary Project offers students a creative and captivating way to work with literary texts while nurturing vital life skills. Students learn by doing. By creating a literature-inspired vacation, students can develop insight into how the background, settings, conflicts, and other literary elements of a novel communicate points of view about life. The project not only enhances literary analysis but also helps students learn basic competencies such as financial planning in a fun, interactive experience that differs completely from other projects. According to Blumenfeld et al. (1991), project-based learning "motivates students to actively construct their understanding by engaging with meaningful problems, creating tangible artifacts, and working collaboratively to deepen their knowledge" (371). The Literary Vacation Itinerary Project does just that.

Email Portfolio: Inbox Impressions

Email etiquette is a valuable lifelong skill that we should intentionally teach and consistently model in our communication with students. I know I'm not alone in having received a cringy student email that contained zero capitalization or spelled *you* as *u*. The goal of the Email Portfolio Project is to teach students how to craft professional and purposeful emails for different audiences and purposes. The project emphasizes essential skills like email etiquette, clear message organization, and audience-appropriate tone to help prepare students for success in both academic and professional settings. For this project, students essentially write an assortment of emails and then compile them into a portfolio to showcase their understanding of how to write emails for different occasions.

1. **Learn about email etiquette.** To begin the project, students need modeled lessons on how to follow proper email etiquette. During this first phrase of the project, students should focus on how to craft a concise and relevant subject line, select proper greetings and closings appropriate to the email's purpose and audience, and modify the tone of voice depending on the audience. Then, in the body of the email, it's important that students learn to be concise, yet clear, and logically structure what they write by following correct email format with an introduction, body, and conclusion. Finally, it's important to emphasize the importance of proofreading for spelling and grammar for polished and professional communication (e.g., no more spelling *you* as *u*). Emails are not text messages, but not all students recognize that, so take time to read and edit different kinds of emails as practice for building up to the portfolio project.

2. **Create emails.** Once students have a clear understanding of how to craft an email that follows basic etiquette, they can begin writing

their collection of emails to compile into a portfolio. Here are the types of emails I like students to include in the portfolio:
- An email to teacher to schedule a make-up assignment
- A follow-up email after a meeting or interview
- An email request for a recommendation letter
- A complaint or concern email
- A job application email

The assortment of emails helps students understand the rhetorical situation and practice adjusting different types of writings to different audiences. This project can and will affect students' lives for years to come. As noted by the Writing Center at the University of North Carolina at Chapel Hill (2025), effective email communication requires consideration of the audience's needs and expectations, which helps in conveying messages appropriately and effectively. If we don't teach them how to write professional emails, then who will? Consider starting the year with this as the first unit to set the expectations for how students should communicate with you and others.

Review Writing: Critic's Corner

As we've discussed, allowing students to express their viewpoints on topics that are of genuine interest to them leads to an increased level of participation, motivation, and attention. Student choice helps students become more invested in their own learning, thereby, increasing the likelihood that students will put forth the effort to produce a high-quality product. As humans, we also like to express our opinions and be heard by others. Taking this part of human nature into consideration, the review essay presents an effective way to give students a voice. The Review Writing Assignment combines student choice with a real-world audience, two of our best ways to engage students in their own learning. After all, some of the most popular types of social media channels are the ones in which people give product reviews. We can use some of these as models for students to write their own reviews.

By writing a review, students learn to evaluate the effectiveness of something and convey this evaluation using evidence and rhetoric to communicate overall quality (or lack thereof). There are lots of things students can review, and by giving them options, they can focus on something that interests them. Here are the types of reviews that typically interest secondary ELA students:

- Restaurant reviews
- Movie or TV show reviews
- YouTube channel reviews
- Game reviews
- Album or song reviews
- App or tech gadget reviews
- Social media account reviews (influencers, celebrities, organizations, etc.)
- Fashion reviews
- Amusement park reviews
- Podcast reviews

Consider allowing students the choice of what they want to review. Alternatively, it can be more approachable for some students to narrow the review options to a specific type. Differentiate this part of the process as needed.

To write a review, one must understand what makes a review engaging and effective. Students build this understanding by analyzing sample reviews and actively participating in collaborative writing exercises to generate and refine review-worthy ideas. Finally, and most importantly students learn to write reviews through the actual writing of a review on a chosen topic. Here are the basic steps for implementing this writing assignment:

1. **Getting started.** Hook students right at the start by showing examples of good reviews versus bad reviews. Ask students to compare the two reviews with questions such as the following:

    - Which review is more effective? Why?
    - Which persuasive devices and techniques does the review use to be convincing?
    - How could the "bad" review be improved? Explain.

    Observing different review essays highlights how an effective review gives insight into the topic, uses evidence and vivid details, and maintains a clear and engaging tone whereas an ineffective review relies more on telling instead of showing and does not use evidence to present a convincing opinion. The more example essays that students read and observe, the more they understand the skills objectives of the assignment. Think about incorporating reviews from sources such as the *New York Times* or *Rolling Stone* for students to annotate and discuss. Published reviews from credible sources make excellent exemplars for this writing task.

2. **Understand structure.** After reviewing model essays, students should dig into the structure of an effective review. To do this, students can observe the essential components of a review such as a clear introduction that hooks the reader and provides relevant background information, body paragraphs that present the writer's opinions with key details backed by evidence and/or examples, an engaging tone that keeps the review interesting and informative, and a conclusion paragraph that presents a rating and/or recommendation (or not). To evidence their understanding of review structure, students can create anchor charts or infographics to

showcase how to write an effective review. They can also highlight and annotate sample essays for organization.

3. **Write the review.** Next, students move through the writing process, beginning with brainstorming ideas and then moving onto outlining, drafting, editing/revision, and finally publication. This process helps reinforce the importance of planning, drafting, and revising to produce effective writing. Students can present their reviews in different ways, either through a printed portfolio, a digital format, or even shared online with their peers through a classroom blog or newsletter, as we discussed previously in the chapter. In addition, students can complete the review assignment in groups and present them to the class.

The Review Writing Assignment not only helps students develop writing skills but also prepares them for real-world tasks such as posting reviews online, giving accurate product feedback, or crafting college or scholarship recommendation letters. It fosters critical thinking, organization, and effective communication in a fun, engaging way. According to Ennis et al. (2020), implementing persuasive writing interventions has been shown to improve both the writing skills and academic engagement of students. That's the goal of this book: to engage learners so that we can help them develop the skills they need to succeed in both academic and real-world contexts.

The Innovative ELA Teacher Pack

Don't forget to access the Innovative ELA Teacher Pack of 50 FREE and EXCLUSIVE resources through the following QR code. Simply follow the QR code over to the Bespoke ELA website to download all 50 FREE resources that accompany the assignments, lessons, activities, and projects found in this book.

Scan the QR code.
Then use the password
JaneAusten1775
to log in and download.

CHAPTER FOUR

Innovative Discussion Strategies

Two cornerstone skills of the English Language Arts (ELA) classroom incorporate speaking and listening. By including innovative discussion strategies, students can work toward mastering speaking and listening while also practicing other important ELA skills such as comprehension, analysis, and supporting claims with evidence. Through discussion, students can learn from each other by being exposed to new ideas and exploring new connections or realizations. Carter et al. (2024) emphasizes that "students must have the opportunity to discuss literature in ways that provoke deep thought and meaning from each work they encounter" (153). Whether students discuss in small groups or with the entire class, giving students an opportunity to be heard in a safe environment helps to build their confidence in speaking and their interest in the content. In this chapter, I share various discussion strategies that resonate with students beyond the scope of the traditional discussion modalities of Socratic seminars.

Defend Your Sequence Discussion

This discussion strategy engages students in a small-group argumentative task where they collaboratively build a logical sequence related to a specific topic or text. Here's how it works:

1. **Get started.** Students receive five cards. This number can be modified as needed. Consider adding more cards to make the game more complex. Each card contains an item such as a quotation, device, topic, character, theme, symbolic object, setting, or conflict.
2. **Arrange the sequence.** Students work in their groups to sequence the cards in an order that makes logical sense to them. For example, five cards for a round over Shakespeare's (2004) tragedy *Macbeth* might include the following cards:
   - **Card 1.** Macbeth
   - **Card 2.** Dagger
   - **Card 3.** "Out, damned spot! out, I say!—One: two: why, then, 'tis time to do't.—Hell is murky!" (Shakespeare 5.1.25–27).
   - **Card 4.** "Life is a tale told by an idiot, full of sound and fury, signifying nothing" (Shakespeare 5.5.17–28).
   - **Card 5.** Blood

   The group then discusses and debates the most logical sequence for the five cards. As groups consider the different options for sequencing the cards, they must defend their ideas with logical reasons and credible evidence.
3. **Present the sequence.** After finalizing their card sequences, each group presents their sequences to the class, explaining their decision-making processes and rationales. A group wins based on the thoroughness, clarity, and logic of their sequence presentation. Award prizes or badges to the winning groups as appropriate.

Helpful Hint: Have more than one sequence deck ready to go so that groups can play multiple rounds as time permits. Also, consider having students create their own cards to add to the sequence deck and then use their cards in one (or more) round(s). Groups can even swap card decks to continue playing.

As an extension to card sequence discussion, I like to have students write a reflective paragraph about the discussion, responding to questions such as these:

- What did you discover from today's discussion?
- What surprised you during the discussion?
- What new connections did you make because of today's discussion?
- What do you still wonder about after the discussion?

Having students reflect on the discussion helps them to solidify their comprehension and understanding of the discussion topic, or text in this case, as well as integrate new ideas and concepts into their own analysis. Rachelle D. Poth (2023) asserts that the act of reflecting on one's experiences significantly sharpens an individual's learning. The adage "you don't know what you don't know" applies to everyone; however, the more we think about our experiences and what we've learned from them, the more we become aware of the potential for growth. Overall, the Defend Your Sequence Discussion gets students to use their analytical thinking skills in an interactive way that keeps them immersed in the content. There's nothing better as a teacher than watching students get into a passionate discussion over literature, and this discussion strategy works well to spark that passion.

Honeycomb Discussions

This discussion technique comes straight from the business world, inspired by the hexagonal discussions that arose during the 1970s as a way for businesses to map out how ideas are connected. Having six sides, the hexagon allows creators to thing about how a topic or item connects in six different ways to other items and topics. In essence, discussion groups use hexagonal tiles to build a web that reveals the interconnectedness of concepts that reflects the complexity of the ideas involved.

In a corporate environment, hexagonal thinking improves strategic decision-making by providing a clear and visual framework for grasping the interplay of different elements. This perspective proves valuable for assessing risk, recognizing opportunities, and crafting strategies (Hulk Apps 2022).

To apply this same concept to secondary ELA and to make it more appealing to students, I've named it the Honeycomb Discussion because it takes inspiration from the hexagonal shape of the honeycomb of a beehive. See Figures 4.1 and 4.2 for an example Honeycomb Discussion about

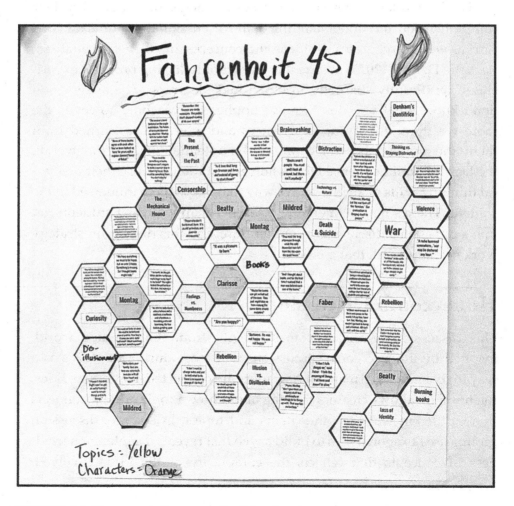

FIGURE 4.1 Honeycomb Discussion for *Fahrenheit 451*.

Innovative Discussion Strategies 79

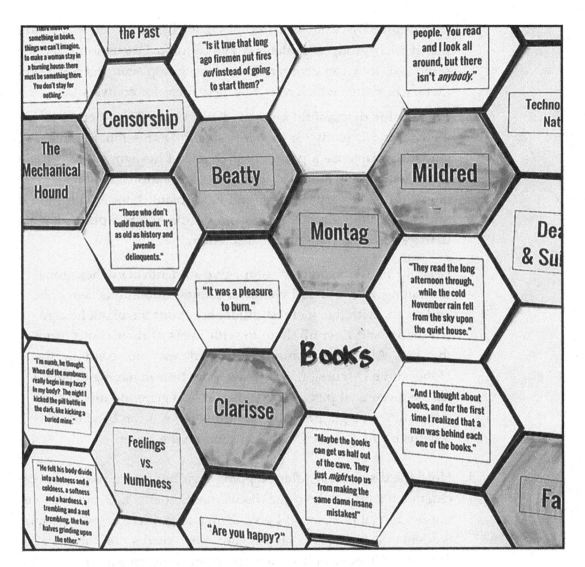

FIGURE 4.2 Honeycomb Discussion for *Fahrenheit 451*—close-up.

Fahrenheit 451. This discussion strategy inspires students to deliberate on a topic or a text to explore the limitless ways that ideas and elements can connect. Here are the steps to implement a Honeycomb Discussion:

1. **Select a topic.** First, the topic of any discussion can be student-selected or teacher-selected. For this discussion strategy, I prefer giving each group the same topic so that they can compare their

Honeycomb Discussions to the ones made by their peers. For example, if each group completes a Honeycomb Discussion over the same text, they can compare how other groups connect ideas and literary elements which can spark new ideas for analysis.

2. **Prepare for discussion.** Give students a prep class period to get their materials ready for the Honeycomb Discussion. On this day, student groups use a packet of pre-created hexagons that contain character names, thematic topics, key quotations, conflicts, symbols, motifs, literary devices, and extra blank honeycomb pieces. Students cut out all their pieces and put them into a plastic baggie to use at the next class for the discussion.

Helpful Hint: For a quicker setup, give students blank hexagonal tiles along with a list of character names, quotations, symbols, and so on. With this method, students cut out the blank hexagonal pieces and then fill them in with items of their choice from the list. Although a more advanced way to conduct the Honeycomb Discussion, it can save prep time in having to create all the hexagonal pieces. Students can also generate this discussion online using a program like Canva, but it can become a bit tedious trying to move shapes around on the screen.

3. **Hold the discussion.** After prepping their hexagonal pieces for discussion, it's time to hold the discussion. Students take out their cut out hexagonal pieces, and I give them a large piece of poster paper. Students then begin laying out the pieces on the paper to form the honeycomb. Because there are so many ways to combine and connect ideas on the hexagonal tiles, students should debate and discuss the best possible layout. To start, each group should select one tile as the centerpiece, which should point to the central message of the text and then build it outward from that central concept. They do not have to use all pieces, but I encourage them to use as many as possible. After completing their Honeycomb Discussions, each group color-codes the elements

on their boards to visually represent how the ideas connect. Students shade their hexagons using the following key: yellow for themes, blue for characters, red for textual evidence, orange for topics, purple for symbols, and green for any additional elements they've included.

4. **Share the discussion.** Once groups are finished with their Honeycomb Discussions, I have them color-code the elements on their discussion boards so that we can visually see how the different elements fit together. Students can color hexagons using the following key: yellow for themes, blue for characters, red for textual evidence, orange for topics, purple for symbols, and green for other elements they added in. Also, students can choose from several follow-up assignments to continue practicing their analytical skills. Consider the following options:

- Hang up the discussion posters around the room and have students conduct a gallery walk. They can take notes on three connections that they hadn't considered for their own Honeycomb Discussions. This helps students expand their comprehension and analysis of the text.

- Have students present their discussion boards to the class by explaining the three most important connections on the board and why they matter to the text.

- Assign an analytical paragraph in which students explain one of the connections from the Honeycomb Discussion Board using textual evidence.

Overall, the Honeycomb Discussion presents another way for students to engage with the material by combining lively discussion and debate through using a visual map of ideas. Through this method, students develop and exhibit critical thinking in a collaborative way that encourages students to participate meaningfully. My students tell me how much they enjoy this different approach to discussing a text. It's definitely worth the effort!

Literary Speed Dating

Literary Speed Dating works to develop students' analytical and critical thinking skills through a fast-moving discussion format about literary elements and techniques. Literary Speed Dating may sound familiar because it's modeled after traditional speed dating. Through this model, students rotate through quick, structured conversations with multiple peers, each focusing on a specific aspect of a text under study. This process helps students become more comfortable speaking with other people they don't know very well. It can also help build confidence in carrying on conversations, a helpful practice to prepare students for future careers.

To prepare for Literary Speed Dating, first decide on how to configure the classroom layout and how the discussion will work. Brian Veprek (2025) states that the speed dating protocol can be modified in different ways to fit various educational environments. The instructor can adjust the timing and frequency of discussions, the classroom setup, the format of the prompts, and, of course, the prompts themselves. I like to construct an inner and outer circle with the inner desks turned to face a desk from the outer circle. This sets up discussion pairs and a simple shape for moving around the room. With this format, the inner circle students are the only ones who get up and rotate.

Give students a Literary Speed Dating handout that contains discussion questions on one side and a space for notes on the other side. The teacher, the students, or both may generate these questions. I like to give students questions that I've written but also have them write some of their own so that they can address aspects of the text or topic that interest or confuse them. It's also important that questions span across the different levels from rote memory to analysis to evaluation and application. Giving students a range of question types helps them move toward higher-level thinking skills and provides the scaffolding to get there. For example, levels of questions over *The Odyssey* could include the following:

- *Level 1* (recall/comprehension): Who is Odysseus, and what is his primary goal in *The Odyssey*?

- *Level 2* (analysis/inference): What does Odysseus's encounter with the Cyclops reveal about his character?
- *Level 3* (evaluation/application): What do Odysseus's challenges and decisions throughout *The Odyssey* suggest about the values of ancient Greek society, and how do those values compare to our current-day values?

Helpful Hint: For differentiation, consider giving students sentence starters to help them begin each new conversation. Sentence starters for discussions can include statements such as the following:

- An important theme I see in the text is _____ as shown by _____.
- I interpret this scene to mean _____ because _____.
- A quote that supports this idea is _____ because _____.

An alternative to using a question sheet could be to give each student a picture that somehow relates to the text. As students rotate to each new conversation, they can share their pictures and discuss how they might relate or how they might reveal themes, conflicts, or character traits. For example, some pictures that teachers could use for a discussion over *The Outsiders* might include the following:

- An image of a gritty urban street or alleyway
- A photo of a classic car from the 1950s
- A photo of a high school clique
- An image of a group of teens engaged in a fight
- A photo of teens from the 1950s with slicked-back hair, leather jackets, and cigarettes in hand

For this option, students can even bring in their own images to spark discussion, making the speed dating format highly adaptable and effective for engaging students with a literary text.

Once students finish preparing for the discussion, here's how the speed dating procedure unfolds:

1. **Get started.** Students take their seats in either the inner or outer circle and prepare to conduct multiple, short, literary discussions with their peers. Emphasize that students need to listen actively, express evidence-based opinions, and reflect on various opinions. Also, be sure to establish ground rules to keep discussions respectful, focused, on topic, and (for the inner circle students) prepared to move to the next partner quickly and quietly. Students can use the text, the discussion guide, and pens/highlighters/sticky notes as needed.

   Helpful Hint: Because students move around the room for this activity, it's a good idea to have them put their backpacks to the side so that no one trips and falls as students rotate during the discussion.

2. **Run the discussion.** Use a timer for each rotation of the discussion to keep the discussion on track. I like to project a timer on the screen so that the whole class can see how much time they have for each round. I typically give students three to five minutes per discussion, but feel free to change this as needed. At the end of each discussion, the inner circle students stand up and rotate to the seat on their right. The clock starts again, and the new pair begins another discussion. As students discuss the text, they can take notes on their key takeaways from each chat and continue through as many rounds as time permits.

3. **Reflect on the discussion.** After the last round, give students a few minutes to write down any final thoughts, insights, or lingering questions they may have in their notebooks or on their discussion notes. Have students reflect on how hearing other interpretations influenced or challenged their original interpretations of the text.

Then, open the discussion to the whole class to reflect on questions such as the following:

- Did anyone change their opinion on a character after hearing others' perspectives?
- What was the most interesting idea that you heard in today's discussion?

4. **Assess the discussion.** To assess the Literary Speed Dating discussion, students can turn in their notes and reflection for a grade. Students can also use ideas from the discussion to write an analytical paragraph about the literary work using textual evidence. I also like to sit in the middle of the inner circle so that I can observe student conversations and take notes on student participation as needed.

Despite its unconventional format, Literary Speed Dating enables students to engage in literature in a collaborative way wherein they can share their interpretations, debate character choices, and consider interpretations from multiple perspectives. Over time, this exercise can help students build confidence to talk to new people and participate in academic conversations. In general, Literary Speed Dating supports students in their development of speaking skills in a lively and meaningful format.

Role-Play Discussion

A Role-Play Discussion operates much like a living museum activity in which students take on the personas of characters, historical figures, or stakeholders as an exercise to discuss different elements of a text from theme to conflict to perspective. Sumaira and Shahzada (2019) state that role-playing lets students use their knowledge in real-life situations, engaging them both mentally and emotionally as they work together to solve problems. Not only does this strategy encourage participation in discussions, but it also allows students to become immersed in the different views, understandings, and interpretations of a text. Although not a new idea, it's still an impactful one. I vividly remember my eighth-grade English teacher asking us to come to school dressed as a historical figure we had researched, then take part in a class interview as that person to share their life story. I came to school as George Gershwin, and a friend of mine came to school as Kurt Cobain. We had to be experts on the person's life to be able to field questions from the class. I will always remember that project because it brought history to life in a way that I'd never experienced. Finding ways to bring experiences to life resonates with students far more than any worksheet or lecture can. While the class interview method combines role-playing with research skills, I prefer adapting the concept into a full-class discussion activity for deeper engagement. That way, the focus shifts to the class and does not spotlight or isolate one student. Here's how to implement a Role-Play Discussion in ELA classes:

1. **Select a discussion question.** The question that drives the discussion determines the people or characters that students select to play. The discussion question should allow for students to take on several different roles from the text or historical event. For example, a discussion question over *The Great Gatsby* could be, "How should we respond to the economic inequality depicted in *The Great Gatsby*?" An example question for an historical event could be, "How did people react to the sinking of the *R.M.S. Titanic* on and off the ship?" Focus on an open-ended question that can bring in different perspectives surrounding the setting and plot to allow for enough roles and points of view.

2. **Decide on roles.** After deciding on the discussion question, students either select a character or real-life person to play during the discussion. The teacher may assign these roles, or students may choose who they want to portray. Consider allowing students to

invent new personas to allow for different perspectives, such as a journalist for the *New York Times* reporting on the public's perception of Jay Gatsby's life and death.

3. **Research the character or person.** Once students know their roles, they can research and prepare by knowing their character's background or historical figure's life story, motivations, relationships, and points of view on key events that occurr during the story or in real life. For literature, this means examining the character's dialogue, actions, and decisions. For real-life figures, this means examining the person's life story, taking note of key accomplishments and life events. As students conduct their research, they should take notes on how their character or person would respond to the discussion question, including quotations and viewpoints. Students can then use their notes during the discussion to help them respond from the perspective of their persona.

4. **Facilitate the discussion.** On the discussion day, students come together to discuss their persona's response to the discussion question. Students are expected to engage in the discussion while staying in character. This means that they need to consider what their character or person knows or does not know about issues, events, or situations. For example, a journalist wouldn't initially know who really killed Jay Gatsby, but could uncover that detail during the discussion and follow up with probing questions to Nick Carraway or Daisy Buchanan—if they're willing to talk. As students respond to each other, the teacher can also add in new questions to keep the discussion dynamic and to assess each student's understanding of their persona's point of view.

Helpful Hint: Have students make nameplates for the discussion to make it easier to keep track of roles. I also like to make sure that I don't have a class with more than one person acting as a main character or historical figure. However, if more than one person plays the same character (i.e., two Jay Gatsby characters), think about having them represent different parts of the story. For instance, assign Gatsby One to take responsibility for everything that happens in the first half of the book, and Gatsby Two for the events in the second half.

5. **Debrief and reflect.** After the discussion, students can drop their roles and reflect on the activity, considering how their views might have changed, what they learned or realized from other perspectives on the discussion topic, and/or how the Role-Play Discussion deepened their understanding of the text or historical event.

Exercises like these are not meant to be gimmicky. Turning a traditional discussion into a Role-Play Discussion comes with added benefits. For one, students learn how to empathize with others by taking on a different perspective, which enables them to experience complex motivations and cultural frameworks. As noted by the Center for Innovative Teaching and Learning (n.d.), "Role playing exercises encourage students to think more critically about complex and controversial subjects and to see situations from a different perspective." Role-playing also helps to promote deeper investigation into themes, conflicts, and character motivations, encouraging students to think analytically and critically to impersonate the voice of someone else. Moreover, the performance aspect of role-play can make the analysis of literature and life events livelier and more memorable, which can help motivate student participation. Using the role-play method with both fiction and nonfiction offers an interactive way of examining life and literature.

Devil's Advocate Game

One of the key competencies of secondary ELA is argumentation. Some authors even argue that all writing is, at its core, an argument—highlighting the importance of rhetorical skills in teaching students how to craft compelling messages for specific audiences. Thus, I made a game

Innovative Discussion Strategies 89

called Devil's Advocate in which students take on the role of the devil's advocate and argue against a set of statements. I use this game mostly as an anticipatory activity at the beginning of a new literary unit to get the class thinking about the big ideas in a text (Dobbs 2017a). Here's how it works:

1. **Get started.** Create a list of debatable statements that correlate to a work of literature. These become the statements that students disagree with throughout the game. See Figure 4.3 for an example list.
2. **Play the game.** Students get into groups, and the teacher reads one statement from the list at a time. Groups then have a set amount of time (say, three to five minutes) to write a one- to two-sentence

Devil's Advocate
ARGUMENT GAME

Schools should ban homework.
Social media does more harm than good.
The legal driving age should be raised to 18.
Celebrities should not be considered role models.
Lying is sometimes necessary.
AI will do more good than harm for society.
Space exploration is a waste of money.
Students should be allowed to grade their teachers.
Athletes and entertainers are overpaid.

FIGURE 4.3 Example list of statements for the Devil's Advocate Game.

response that disagrees with the topic. They can start the statement with the sentence like: "I couldn't disagree more because … ." For instance, in response to the statement, "Ambition leads to corruption" for a unit on Shakespeare's play *Macbeth,* a group could formulate a Devil's Advocate response that says, "I strongly disagree, as ambition does not corrupt every character in the play—Banquo, for instance, remains honorable despite his ambitions." Through this practice, students get to explore the other side of a topic or issue that they might not have considered previously while simultaneously practicing rhetorical skills.

3. **Score points.** Next, each group shares their Devil's Advocate statement with the whole class. As each group shares, they can earn a point for crafting a statement that includes a valid reason and logical rationale. If a group cannot come up with a statement in the time allotted, they lose a point instead. Once each group has shared their Devil's Advocate statements, the whole class can discuss the statement and vote on the group that had the most convincing disagreement. The group that wins the vote can earn an additional point. Work through as many rounds as time permits. At the end, the group with the most points wins the game!

Helpful Hint: Consider having each group designate one person as the speaker and one person as the group's reporter to avoid confusion. Additionally, groups should not be allowed to vote for their own statements to make the game fair.

After the game, students can complete an exit ticket to reflect on how the game challenged, changed, or confirmed something they believed. Students walk away from this discussion game with new insights and enjoy the challenge of disagreeing with something they might have originally believed to be true. The Devil's Advocate Game provides another interactive strategy for students to improve their argumentation skills (Dobbs 2017a).

Around the World Discussion

This discussion technique offers a simple setup and easy moderation. It formalizes the process to ensure every student has a chance to speak while promoting active listening. However, the challenge in this type of discussion is to avoid repeating what anyone else says. This takes paying attention and thinking critically to delve deeper into a question and use evidence to support claims.

Here are the basics rules of how to hold an Around the World Discussion. The name essentially states how this discussion strategy works: students get into a circle and answer a question one-by-one in a round robin fashion. Remember that students should aim not to repeat what anyone else says, which requires that they pay close attention and listen actively during discussion. The two most basic ways for students to respond are to agree or disagree with other students' comments. However, a student may also steer the discussion in a new direction, as long as that shift stays purposeful and relevant. It should fit organically into the context of the discussion.

To keep the discussion moving and to help students if they can't think of a new comment, I allow them three lifelines to use as needed. These lifelines include the following:

- A question mark that gives the student the option to pose a new question to take the conversation in a new direction
- A pass that allows students to skip a turn
- A repeat sign (like the musical annotation) that permits a student one chance to repeat an idea already mentioned in the discussion by another peer

To keep track of these lifelines, I give students three sticky notes to hang on the front of their desks. As a student uses a lifeline, they remove the sticky note from the desk to signify that they have used it.

Helpful Hint: Feel free to add in more lifelines as needed. I like to put surprise booster sticky notes underneath a few desks at random for students to find that give those students an extra pass or the opportunity to reverse the direction of the discussion and skip a turn. These lifelines keep the discussion lively and interactive.

What if a student reaches a point where they have used up all their lifelines and still can't think of a unique comment? Although this doesn't happen often, it's generally a sign that the student either has not read the text or was not adequately prepared for discussion. These students can shift into a listener-notetaker role for the remainder of the discussion and must follow up with the teacher afterwards. Rather than grade these students on their spoken participation in the discussion, I have them turn in their notes instead to receive partial credit.

There are so many ways to make class discussions interactive and engaging for students, and this discussion approach supports learners— whether they came to class prepared or not. It allows for active listening, critical thinking, and reflective thought as students take turns sharing their analysis with the class. As stated by the Taylor Institute for Teaching and Learning (2025), the methods of effective discussion-based teaching can lead to improvements in some rather important skills— namely, critical thinking, problem-solving, and comprehension of diverse viewpoints. The round the World Discussion exposes students to the varied options that come with literary analysis. It's an inclusive activity that students begin to enjoy and own with repeated practice.

The Innovative ELA Teacher Pack

Don't forget to access the Innovative ELA Teacher Pack of 50 FREE and EXCLUSIVE resources through the following QR code. Simply follow the QR code over to the Bespoke ELA website to download all 50 FREE resources that accompany the assignments, lessons, activities, and projects found in this book.

Scan the QR code.
Then use the password
JaneAusten1775
to log in and download.

CHAPTER FIVE

Innovative Literary Activities for Any Novel

Engaging students in literary analysis works more effectively when we move beyond the traditional approaches of worksheets and essays. According to Smith and Jones (2017), "When students engage in creative, project-based tasks such as designing new endings or reimagining scenes, they not only deepen their analytical skills but also find personal relevance in the literature they study" (151). This chapter focuses on helping teachers develop versatile techniques that breathe new life into literary analysis and instruction through activities that can work for any genre and skill level across a range of texts. Students can apply these strategies to everything from classic literary works to contemporary fiction—even to novels they select themselves. To sustain interest and motivation, we must approach assessment with flexibility and creativity.

This chapter offers a toolkit of innovative literary activities designed to help students explore a text's deeper thematic meaning, regardless of the novel or classroom setting. The goal is to take students beyond worksheets and reading quizzes and turn students into avid readers, thinkers, and creators. Here are some unique ideas to do that.

Novel Expressions

This activity turns literary analysis into an artistic, hands-on experience that challenges students to build art installations that depict key themes, symbols, characters, and/or conflicts of literary work. It engages secondary ELA students by merging analysis with artistic expression for deeper comprehension of a text. Todd Kettler (2020) emphasizes that "the discipline of language arts is also a component of the humanities tradition—the process of creating and performing through reading, writing, speaking, and listening." By taking a humanities-driven approach to literary analysis, combined with creativity, we can expand our students' cultural horizons.

> *Helpful Hint*: Since many of my students are of driving age, I turn this activity into a "trunk-or-treat" style artistic installation, where each group transforms a member's car trunk into an immersive exhibit representing their literary work. However, this can be done anytime of the year, and students don't have to use car trunks. They can set up their Novel Expressions in the classroom, hallways, library, or online.

But why an art project when this isn't an art class? I've heard this question from my students, and I've heard it from other English teachers as well. Using a humanities-driven project challenges students to make connections between art and literature. Making connections pulls us into the world of the text and enables us to appreciate the literary work in relation to our lives and the world around us. Kathy G. Short (n.d.) points out that "in their daily lives, learners constantly make connections across past and present experiences in order to construct their understandings of themselves and their world" (1). This process involves making connections to art in order to enlighten new interpretations of a text.

For instance, recognizing our own struggles in a work of literature fosters a deeper emotional connection to the text but also helps us to empathize more with a character's situation and conflict. This philosophy drives the Novel Expressions Project. I think it's also important to allow space in an English curriculum for all types of learners to find success. This project engages the visual and kinesthetic learners who might not do as well with a traditional essay or presentation project. It also comes with the added benefit of making abstract concepts more concrete and the learning experience more memorable and meaningful. Here's how it works:

1. **Create a thesis statement.** At the end of a novel unit, after students have analyzed the novel's themes, symbols, characters, and conflicts, assign student groups the task of crafting a focused thesis statement. This thesis statement should contain a literary argument (theme) as shown through a character shift and a symbol in the story. For example, a thesis statement for *To Kill a Mockingbird* might be: "In *To Kill a Mockingbird*, Harper Lee uses the symbol of the mockingbird and the character shift in Scout's understanding of morality to illustrate how prejudice destroys innocence and how empathy can help us overcome societal injustices."

2. **Create a mood board.** Designers then use mood boards to construct the overall mood, tone, impression, and concept of an artistic design before launching into making specific pieces. Their mood boards can include sketches, diagrams, color swatches, fonts, pictures, quotes, and written explanations—essentially anything that would help them develop the final product. See Figure 5.1 for an example mood board for *To Kill a Mockingbird*.

   Helpful Hint: As we all know, it's important to establish checkpoints for multistep projects so that we can help students stay on track. At this point, I meet with groups to review their mood boards and help them troubleshoot any issues with their project plans. I also work with groups on how to source what they need and construct what they want to make. Sometimes, this involves helping students scale down their ideas to make them more practical for the space available at school.

98   Bespoke ELA

FIGURE 5.1 Mood board example for the Novel Expressions Project.

3. **Create the art installation**. This project can be big or small (physically) depending on the space available at school. Learners can even complete the project online using Canva or Google Slides. Determine how best to implement this project for your learners and go from there. Here are some Novel Expressions art installation ideas from some of my past students:

   • One group explained the sense of injustice in *To Kill a Mockingbird* by creating a diorama of a courtroom scene with a broken scale of justice on top to point out the disequilibrium caused by prejudice in the novel.

   • Another group created three paintings that represented Don Quixote's shift in character from obsession with idealism to surrendering to reality.

- Another group made a photo wall of original photography that showcased key tones, quotes, moods, and themes from *Frankenstein*.

Consider having students add a QR code to their Novel Expressions art exhibits that links to a written explanation of the project. The written component can help viewers understand how the art installation connects to a text, and it can help fellow students engage with literature on a deeper level—not to mention that seeing a crowd of students clicking on a QR code can pique student interest in the projects and involve the entire school in literature in an entirely new way.

Essentially, students craft an artistic museum exhibit that relates literature to artistic expression, a powerful way to express analysis and understanding of a text's nuances. Connecting literature and art amplifies the learning journey by nurturing creativity, boosting critical thinking, and clarifying understanding. As noted by Learning Through Literature (n.d.), "One of the biggest benefits of combining art and literature is the way it helps students improve their reading comprehension and critical thinking skills." This project helps different senses to work together and leads to a deeper understanding of the text, especially in comprehension of character and themes.

Character's Contents Project

For this project students analyze a character from a novel, play, short story, or epic poem and use physical objects that showcase important traits of that character. Students should consider the character's physiology (physical attributes), sociology (background and upbringing), and psychology (behavioral traits). The physical objects of the project should metaphorically represent these aspects as well as how the character shifts or changes from the beginning of the story to the end—all backed by textual evidence. Framing character analysis through physical objects helps students to abstract thematic meaning from concrete items. In addition, using physical objects helps students think more closely about a character's motivations, conflicts, personality, and journey. Basically, students collect items to use as a means for analyzing a character by explaining how those items showcase different aspects of the character.

While the idea of analyzing a character through their belongings isn't entirely new, using creative and engaging "containers" can add a fresh twist. Students consider what their character might pack and explore what each item reveals about their personality, motivations, and relationships. Some container ideas include the following:

- Suitcase
- Christmas stocking
- Time capsule
- Locker
- Treasure chest
- Survival kit
- Scrapbook
- Jewelry box
- Time traveler's backpack

There are lots of other ways for students to present a character's contents other than these. Encourage students to brainstorm their own ideas for how they would like to present a character's belongings to the class.

In addition, this activity makes character analysis more interesting due to its practical and creative approach. Rather than writing essays, filling out worksheets, or making another body map, students can take on an active role in using a more interesting form to communicate their analysis, helping students to approach the work with imagination. This approach makes literary analysis more engaging, especially when exploring characterization. Remember that student buy-in can yield better student efficacy and overall better results. Here are the basic steps for implementing the project:

1. **Get started.** Students begin with a character from a novel, short story, play, or epic poem—either assigned by the teacher or selected by the students.

2. **Gather artifacts.** Students then begin to analyze the character by selecting, finding, or creating items that represent the character's personality, motivations, and development. The number of items each group selects may vary, but starting with around five provides a solid foundation. These items serve as tools to analyze and present the character's traits, conflicts, and overall growth in a creative and engaging way. Students then curate the items so that they embody key aspects of the character and put them into a container of some sort that also connects to the character's story. Teachers can opt to give students the choice of how to pack their character's contents or assign all students to use the same one, such as a suitcase. Here are some project options:

   - A suitcase filled with items representing a character's journey and ambitions
   - A Christmas stocking full of symbolic gifts that reflect the character's desires or sorrows
   - A time capsule filled with objects the character might want to preserve for the future
   - A memory box with items representing foundational experiences or relationships

3. **Analyze Items.** After students compile their character's items, they write an analysis explaining how each item connects to the character's traits and overall story arc supported by textual evidence.

4. **Present to the class.** Once students have prepared their character's objects and written the analysis for each one, it's time to present them to the class. Consider these presentation options:
   - **Show-and-tell.** Students explain each item and how it relates to the character.
   - **Gallery walk.** Students put their projects on display, and their classmates circulate to each station to explore the contents. At each station, students can open the container to explore the contents and discuss how each item connects to the character in the story.
   - **Video presentation.** Students can make a video that explains their character's contents to the class. This option works efficiently for groups that know they will have a group member absent on the project due date.
   - **In-character presentation.** A student can come to class and act as the character to present the contents. My thespian students really like this option.

Students absolutely love this project. It gives them an entirely different method for analyzing character. The project not only reinforces textual analysis but also brings the complexity of literature to life in a tangible, approachable way—making it more engaging for all students, including neurodivergent learners. It also helps to foster an appreciation of symbolism and metaphor as students seek to find physical objects that represent the abstract ideas of a text. It is a great project for all types of learners.

What's on Your Plate? Character Analysis

In this activity, a paper plate functions as a metaphor for a character's hardships, struggles, and/or defining traits. The purpose is to answer the question, "What's on your character's plate at this point in the story?" It leans heavily on the idiomatic expression, "I've got a lot on my plate right now." Here are the steps for implementing this activity with any character from any text.

1. **Get started.** Begin by discussing the meaning and purpose of a metaphor. This helps students understand that the paper plate represents, in essence, a character's feelings, burdens, problems, and conflicts at a given point in a story. It is a physical way to help students see and understand a character's situation.

   Helpful Hint: Consider having students complete this activity about their own lives and what's on their plates at the current moment. This project introduction not only helps students express and process stressors in their own lives but also provides students with a model to use for the character part of the project.

   By turning abstract ideas into a physical representation, students can better empathize with a character and make predictions about what will become of that character. To get them started, students should consider the conflicts, emotions, problems, and adversities the character faces at a precise moment in a story. Then, they should represent each detail about the character on the plate by using symbolic doodles, images, words, 3D elements, colors, and quotations.

2. **Create the plate.** Provide students with paper plates, markers, colored pencils, and other art supplies they can use to create their character plates. To help students complete this activity, have them divide the paper plate into sections—or not. This is where differentiation matters. Some student groups may not need any directives to help them structure the assignment while others might need

specific sections and requirements. When using sections, consider including the following aspects:

- **Character background.** Include any information about the character's past that relates to the character's difficulties and adversities in the story.
- **Important relationships.** Consider the relationships that are important to the character and how these relationships either help or harm the character.
- **Difficulties or adversities.** Add symbols, and images that showcase the character's adversities.
- **Responsibilities or tasks.** Think about what the character must do in the story and how that creates problems for the character.
- **Internal and external conflicts.** Use colors, shapes, or patterns to represent emotional turmoil and external pressures.
- **Emotions and behaviors.** Depict how the character's situation affects his or her feelings and actions or responses to others.
- **Theme.** Identify the dominant theme associated with the character's journey. Write the theme and include a symbol that represents the character's main life lesson.
- **Textual evidence.** Include direct quotations with MLA parenthetical citations to support each section of the plate. Each quotation should clearly connect to each section of the plate.

3. **Create meaningful elements.** Encourage students to use the visual elements also as metaphors or symbols for different aspects of the character. Students can include doodles, colors, borders, and 3D elements to represent key characteristics. For example, a red border around the plate could represent passion or anger. A doodle of a clock could represent the pressure of time. A crumbled piece of paper glued to the plate could represent a mistake. Students can use their imaginations to make the plate as symbolic as possible, furthering the creative and analytical challenge of the activity.

Innovative Literary Activities for Any Novel   **105**

4. **Write the explanation.** On the back of the plate, or elsewhere (Google Doc, separate sheet of paper, etc.), have students then write a description of the items on the plate, explaining how the visual and textual elements represent the character's traits and struggles. Students can also predict what they think will happen to the character given the issues the character faces. See Figure 5.2 for a student example.

FIGURE 5.2 Student example of the What's on Your Plate? activity.

5. **Present the analysis.** Finally, students can present their plates to small groups and/or the entire class. This activity can also serve as a preparation activity for a graded discussion, using the guiding question: "Who or what is to blame for the character's problems?" Students can use the information on their plates to support their responses during the discussion. This activity offers a creative and effective way to prepare, while also lending itself to other formats for sharing. Blending creativity with analysis helps spark engagement and deepen motivation..

Helpful Hint: Consider passing out random plates to groups and allowing them to analyze how the plate represents a character's problems and adversities. Groups can continue swapping and discussing plates as time permits. This takes them to the evaluation level of learning and exposes them to new ideas and interpretations for reflection.

The What's on Your Plate? activity enables students to tap into a character's inner world in a creative and symbolic way. It visually shows what fills up a character's plate of problems, responsibilities, struggles, and emotions. This characterization explores how external pressures shape a character's actions and decisions in the development of a story, fostering both empathy and critical thinking in a meaningful way. Creative activities like the What's on Your Plate? Project can work to engage students in theme analysis and make the literature more memorable and meaningful.

Character Trial Project: Justice in Literature

Although not a brand-new idea, putting a character on trial always makes for an interactive and dynamic way to involve students in literature. This project encourages critical thinking, persuasive speaking, collaborative teamwork, and literary analysis all while teaching students about the justice system. According to Facing History & Ourselves (2025), "Putting the characters through a mock trial not only enables students to re-examine the text in depth and develop their argument-building skills, it also introduces them to the notion of justice." To implement this project, students put a character from literature on trial for a specific "crime" they commit in a work of literature. Through this project, students can further develop their understanding of character motivations and conflicts found in a story. Here are the steps for implementing a Character Trial Project:

1. **Learn about trials.** To begin, students need to learn about the people in the courtroom during a trial and what each person does. They also need to learn about how a trial works in terms of structure, timing, and organization. This ensures that students are prepared for the project and have a broad understanding of how a trial works in real life. Students can construct an outline of the order of trial to use as a guideline during the project. This helps the trial project run more smoothly. Teachers can modify the trial schedule as needed to fit class period times. The following steps include the basic framework for the trial:

   - **Prosecution's opening statement.** (5–10 minutes) The prosecution outlines their case and explains how they will show evidence that proves the defendant is guilty.

   - **Defense's opening statement.** (5–10 minutes) The defense gets a turn to outline their case and explain why the defendant is innocent.

   - **Presentation of prosecution's case.** (30–60 minutes) The prosecution calls witnesses to testify as to why the defendant is guilty. During testimonies, the prosecution can present evidence.

   Helpful Hint: So that everyone in the classroom/courtroom can see the evidence that the attorneys present in their cases, I require that they make a Google Slideshow to showcase their exhibits. That way, during the trial, we can shine a piece of evidence on the screen for everyone to see. However you decide to handle the evidence, make sure that everyone has access to it—even if it's a printed packet.

To keep the process more basic for our students, after the prosecution asks their questions for each witness, the defense gets a chance to cross-examine the witness (or ask their own questions of the witness). We skip the witness redirect due to time constraints, but if you have more time, go for it!

- **Presentation of defense's case.** (30–60 minutes) The defense then gets a turn to call their own witnesses, and the prosecution gets to cross-examine each one.
- **Closing arguments.** (5–10 minutes for each side) Both sides take a turn summarizing their cases, highlighting the key points and evidence they showed through their witnesses.
- **Jury instructions.** The judge speaks to the jury and asks them to consider everything they've heard and to make their decision based on the burden of evidence "beyond a reasonable doubt."
- **Jury deliberation.** (20–30 minutes) Unlike the real world, where juries can take as long as they need to deliberate the verdict of a case, we cannot because we are pressed for time. As a result, I give the jury about 30 minutes maximum to arrive at a verdict and deliver it to the judge.
- **Verdict announcement.** The judge announces the verdict of the jury and closes the trial.
- **Sentencing.** If the jury finds the defendant guilty, the judge determines the appropriate punishment for the crime.

Helpful Hint: Setting time limits for each part of the trial keeps the trial on track. Consider projecting a timer like they do in some real-life courtrooms so that everyone can keep track of time limits.

2. **Choosing the literary crime and the defendant.** It is important to choose the crime committed by a character from a text the class has already read and analyzed. By choosing a familiar work of literature, students can draw on their knowledge and understanding of the text to engage thoughtfully in the trial process. Here are a few examples of literary characters and crimes to consider using for this project:

   - Friar Lawrence—or even Lord Montague and Lord Capulet—could be put on trial for their culpability in the deaths of Romeo and Juliet.
   - Victor Frankenstein could be put on trial for his culpability in the deaths of William Frankenstein, Henry Clerval, Justine Moritz, Elizabeth Lavenza, and/or Alphonse Frankenstein.
   - Jack could be put on trial for his culpability in the deaths of Piggy and Simon.
   - Odysseus could be put on trial for the deaths of his men and the suitors.
   - Daisy Buchanan could be put on trial for murdering Myrtle.

   After selecting a case, students can begin to apply for their roles in the trial.

3. **Assign roles and tasks.** Students then submit their top three desired roles for trial, including explanations to explain why they are a good fit for each one. Roles can include the following:

   - **The judge.** Played by the teacher, student, or another adult (could even be a volunteer parent)
   - **Prosecuting attorneys.** (2–4 students) Argue the character's guilt
   - **Defense attorneys.** (2–4 students) Argue the character's innocence
   - **Jury members.** (10–12 students) Listen to the case and decide on the guilt or innocence of the character based on the evidence presented at trial

- **Witnesses.** (4–6 students) Act out parts of characters in the story and testify based on their involvement in the story
- **Media.** (4–6 students) Watch the trial and report on key events
- **Bailiff.** (1 student) Maintains order and safety in the courtroom and handles documents
- **Optional roles.** Courtroom artist, courtroom photographer, exhibit creator, tech person

Each students' role in the trial has its own specific set of requirements for the Character Trial Project. Once I have read each student's application, I assign roles accordingly and give each student a file folder for their designated role. The folder contains the steps, instructions, assignments, and tasks for each student to complete. For instance, a juror will take notes during the trial, participate in deliberating the verdict, and then write a persuasive essay to explain their vote based on evidence presented at trial and in the text. Essentially, each student role involves taking notes and completing a written assignment that differs based on the student's role in the trial. Throughout the trial, students also receive participation daily grades based on paying attention, fulfilling their duties, and participating in a meaningful way.

4. **Research and prepare for trial.** Before trial, students need time to research and prepare for their roles. These instructions and tasks are provided in each student folder. Prosecution and defense teams need to prepare their opening and closing statements and write questions for the witnesses. They should be prepared to use textual evidence from the story as the basis for constructing their arguments. Witnesses write witness statements based on their actions in the text to construct a testimony that captures the essence of their characters. For example, Daisy Buchanan would probably not be very honest and forthcoming in being the one who kills Myrtle in *The Great Gatsby*. Witnesses testify in character, drawing on their

experiences and perspectives from the story (great for student thespians). Students who take on observer roles such as the bailiff and members of the media or jury can do more research into court procedures or past cases to better prepare them for the trial.

5. **Create the courtroom.** Morph the classroom into a courtroom. I have a podium, so I use that as the judge's seat. I also wear an old graduation robe and use a pretend gavel I bought on Amazon to play the part of the judge. As the judge, I'm able to observe everyone in the classroom and keep track of participation and attention. I divide the class into the sections of a courtroom—a chair beside me for the witnesses, two tables up front for the prosecution and defense, seats at the back for the media, and seats on the side for the jury. The more lifelike the setup, the more students tend to engage with the process.

6. **Conduct the trial.** We move through the trial outline, step-by-step, but we maintain a level of reasonable flexibility in case a specific part needs more time. Before the trial days, we talk about how to dress for court, and I award bonus points on the daily participation grade for students who dress the part. This helps in making the atmosphere more believable. Once the case has settled, and the judge turns the decision over to the jury, I rearrange the classroom to place the jury in the middle of the room. The rest of the class gets to listen in on their discussion and take notes although they cannot speak or react while the jury deliberates. Allowing the class to hear the jury deliberate the verdict helps everyone observe how the members of the jury interpreted what they heard during trial. When the jury is ready, they present the verdict, and the judge orders the sentencing. Consider using local or state laws to guide the punishment phase, which can help learners better understand the legal system where they live.

7. **Reflect and discuss.** After the trial is over, we discuss the entire experience as a class, and students write a one-page reflection of what they learned, discovered, or found interesting about the legal

process and the central text of the project. Undoubtedly, students emerge from this project having gained more insight into the characters, themes, and moral issues presented by the text. Students then finish up the remaining assignments from their trial folders and submit for grading.

The Character Trial Project actively involves students in collaborative, real-life learning that integrates several ELA skills. The trial simulation transforms the classroom into a vibrant setting that puts students at the center of their own learning and enables them to consider literary elements such as perspective and point of view, develop strong arguments, and use textual evidence to persuade their peers. Using the backdrop of a real-world courtroom, coupled with the chance to put a character on trial, students tend to buy in to the literature in a more interactive way. According to Shane Safir (2015), "Mock trials are a gap-closing strategy. By engaging students in rigorous and authentic literacy tasks, trials demand high levels of critical thinking, critical reading, and persuasive writing." They not only bring about an increased understanding of literature but also help students examine the moral and ethical qualities of characters from a text in a context that is radically different from a traditional class.

Literary NFT Gallery

Let's start this project off with a little tech talk about NFTs. An NFT is a non-fungible token. These objects began to materialize during the early to mid-2010s along with blockchain technology but took off in 2017 when creators gained the capability through Ethereum's smart contracts to give their tokens unique, artistic attributes (NFT now 2021). CryptoPunks and CryptoKitties started to become popular as NFT artists, and even today, NFTs are still a significant means for proving ownership of digital and even physical assets. This movement led to the rapid growth of digital art, and its popularity increased to the point that Beeple sold an NFT for $69 million through Christie's Auction House (NFT now 2021). It's an incredible collage and worth looking up online.

So, how can we use NFT technology as a concept for analyzing literature? In this project, students design a virtual gallery of literary NFTs in response to a work of literature. Each NFT represents a character, theme, or symbol in the text, combining visual art with literary analysis as students examine ways in which digital media can provide commentary of literature. If their NFTs are good enough, students could even opt to sell them online. Here's how students can create NFTs as a means for analyzing literature:

1. **Learn about NFTs.** To get started with this activity, students should spend some time learning about NFTs. The non-fungible describes something that cannot be exchanged, which is unlike fungible cryptocurrency that can be exchanged. Each NFT has unique metadata that proves ownership, making them like digital keys that protect assets (NFT now 2021). They act as unique, verifiable proof of ownership for any digital or physical asset that cannot be duplicated. But what makes them valuable? They serve as proof of ownership, and because they are one-of-a-kind, their scarcity creates demand. Students can explore NFTs online to see how they can encapsulate art, music, videos, or any other form of media to make them unique. Students can look up examples from top NFT creators such as Bored Ape Yacht Club, Beeple, or CryptoPunks to get an idea of what they can look like. Once students understand NFTs, they can apply this concept to analyzing a text.

2. **Choose a text.** Next, students need to choose a novel, play, epic poem, or short story that they have studied in class. Similar to other literary activities and projects, teachers may choose to assign a common text to the entire class or offer students the opportunity to select their own. After they select a text, students can get into

groups and begin designing mockups of NFT ideas that connect to the work of literature. Encourage students to practice with different styles from abstract creations to photo collages.

3. **Select literary elements.** In this step, students select a theme that comes through the story's symbolism and characterization. For example, for *Their Eyes Were Watching God* by Zora Neale Hurston, students might choose the theme, "The pursuit of self-discovery leads to personal freedom." For a symbol, they could select something like the pear tree, Janie's hair, or the gate, and for characterization, Janie could be characterized as independent, resilient, and reflective. The NFT should incorporate these elements and techniques to clearly highlight the connection between its design and the literary text.

4. **Mint NFTs.** After identifying literary elements, students can begin the process of creating their NFTs as digital artwork that visually depicts the chosen elements. Students can use free design tools such as Canva, Adobe Spark, Google Drawings, or Pixlr (a free online photo editor). Consider giving students the option to use AI generators or scan hand-drawn designs to create their digital images. Students can experiment with the different style methods (collage, abstract, literal) to help them decide which direction to take. For example, a neon green lighthouse could represent Gatsby's dreams and obsessions in The Great Gatsby, while a broken crown might symbolize Macbeth's downfall, driven by his unchecked ambition. Essentially, students can use the NFT platform to produce a digital image inspired by a text that presents analysis of key literary elements.

5. **Add metadata.** Metadata is the embedded, descriptive information that conveys the details surrounding an NFT and the asset it represents. The metadata makes every NFT unique. It usually includes the unique name of the NFT, a brief description of its meaning and attributes—such as color analysis, accessories, art

style, or rarity (Pastel Network 2021)—and keywords to enhance searchability. To make this relevant for literary analysis in English Language Arts (ELA), students can build the NFT metadata on the analysis of a work of literature and include a 500-word essay that analyzes the theme depicted in their unique NFT. Here's an example of what that could look like using Shakespeare's play *Romeo and Juliet* (2004):

Name. *Romeo and Juliet: Impulse and Tragedy*

Description. This NFT represents a student interpretation of William Shakespeare's play *Romeo and Juliet*. The analysis explores the theme that acting upon emotions leads to downfall. Accompanied by a creative visual depiction, this digital artwork showcases literary analysis and artistic expression.

Image. URL that points to the NFT image

Attributes. This NFT sheds light on the important moments in the play when hasty decisions lead to devastating consequences, including a secret marriage, the death of Tybalt, and the tragic outcome for the two lovers. The visual work features a digital painting of a shattered rose, symbolizing the beauty of love and passion destroyed by rash actions. The shattered rose set against a dual-toned background of red represents passion while black represents tragedy and death. The NFT includes the quote, "These violent delights have violent ends" surrounded by flames to represent the destructive force of passion as depicted in the play (Shakespeare 2004, 2.6.9). See Figure 5.3 for a depiction of this NFT.

Keywords. Romeo and Juliet, passion, Shakespeare, tragedy, star-crossed lovers, literary analysis, English

Literary analysis. Although not part of NFT listings, for the sake of English class, students can craft a 500-word literary analysis of the theme depicted in the NFT design.

FIGURE 5.3 NFT inspired by Shakespeare's *Romeo and Juliet*.

6. **Create a mock NFT art gallery.** Once students have created their NFTs and metadata, they can compile them into an NFT art gallery, uploading their artwork and metadata on a platform such as Google Slides, Padlet, or Wakelet to mimic a real-life NFT marketplace. A site called OpenSea is the largest NFT platform online, and students can look there for inspiration and ideas not only for creating their own NFTs but also for what the NFT marketplace looks like.

Helpful Hint: Students could consider how to put their NFTs up for sale, and their classmates could take part in a mock auction to bid on them. Students could also explore real-life NFT tools on platforms such as Minting of NFTs or Tezos.

The task of creating NFTs to analyze literature enables students to blend modern technology with analysis in an artistic way. Moreover, exploring non-fungible tokens involves a new way of looking at digital ownership, expanding students' appreciation for literature while also enabling our students to engage with 21st-century, marketable skills.

Podclassics: A Literary Podcast Project

Podcasts are all the rage, and we can use this popular platform in ELA to engage in literary analysis in a collaborative format. Sandy Scragg (2022) writes, "Creating podcasts with your middle and high school students isn't just a trendy project; it's a task that checks many important boxes: using real-world skills, applying content knowledge, integrating technology, learning and practicing English for English language learners, incorporating student voice, practicing all components of English language arts and meeting the Next Generation Learning Standards." Therefore, podcasts can be a powerful tool in ELA classes.

For this project, students essentially produce a podcast episode to discuss important aspects of a text—either teacher-selected or student-selected. The podcast should demonstrate analytical thinking, knowledge, comprehension, and creativity. It should be a scripted, planned, and organized conversation about a piece of literature (or nonfiction issue) created by students, for students. Here are the key steps for implementing this project:

1. **Introduce podcasts.** To introduce students to podcasts, begin by listening to episodes of student-friendly podcasts such as *The Past and the Curious*, *True*, or even something more daring like *Crime Junkie* (prescreening required). As students listen to each episode, they should observe the structure of how the podcast host(s) present information and how they hold the listeners' attention. Students should also focus on the key elements that make for an effective podcast. For example, students can listen to a more conversational

episode and a script-read episode (like many from *Wondery*) to compare/contrast how the different styles of delivery affect the listener's experience. They can also assess the tone, mood, and energy of the host(s) to assess the podcast's overall attitude—whether it is serious, humorous, or enthusiastic—and how the tone correlates to the podcast topic. Students should also observe the overall structure that includes a catchy introduction with the podcast title, subtitle, teaser, and jingle. Generally speaking, the introduction comes first, followed by the narrative of the episode, and ends with a memorable conclusion. As students listen to podcast episodes, they should make observations about the creative techniques of the production such as the use of sound, music, cliff-hangers, or questions that keep the audience interested and connected. After making their observations, students can reflect on how these features have an impact on listener interest and then apply these same elements to their own podcasts. Here are some questions for students to consider during this introductory part of the project:

- How does the host's tone of voice sound? Serious? Funny? Excited?
- How does the tone make the podcast engaging?
- What is the order of the podcast?
- Does it start with an introduction? Include a main discussion? End with an effective closing?
- What techniques keep the audience engaged? Do the hosts use questions, humor, sound effects, music, suspense, and so on?

2. **Create the podcast episode.** The following steps guide students through the process of creating their own podcast—from planning and scripting to recording and publishing. Groups bring the project to life by following these steps:
    - Invent a catchy podcast title and subtitle that relates to the selected work of literature.

- Find a jingle and other musical elements or sound effects to use throughout the production
- Write the script of the podcast episode, which should include the following sections:
  - Introduction to the work of literature
  - Interesting biographical information about the author and historical time period or setting of the text
  - Introduction to the main characters along with a brief biography of each one
  - Short plot summary of key events in the story
  - Analysis of key themes with textual evidence and thoughtful insights about how literary elements and devices such as characterization, conflict, irony, or symbolism communicate the overall messages
  - A conclusion that includes the group's recommendation opinions

Although this organizational structure presents a straightforward approach to the PodClassics Project, there are alternative, high-interest options for students to explore beyond the scope of traditional literary analysis. For example:

- **Character interviews.** For this podcast idea, students take on the personas of characters from the text and come onto the podcast as guests for an interview about their story, diving into their motivations, challenges, and backgrounds.
- **Alternate endings.** In this podcast concept, students can brainstorm alternate endings to the story and then discuss which one they like best in terms of characters and plot.
- **Literary debate.** This option brings the debate to the podcast. Instead of having students debate a work of literature in class, they can do it on the podcast. They can respond to a yes/no

debate question with a group of students live on the air to talk through the different points that support both sides of the argument using textual evidence.

- **Book versus movie.** For this angle, students analyze the cinematic elements of a movie adaptation, comparing and evaluating how the film interprets the book.
- **Villain's defense.** Here, students argue whether the villain is misunderstood and defend the villain's actions in the story. It's a way of looking at a villain as an antihero rather than simply classifying the villain as purely evil.
- **Top five lists.** With this prompt, students share different top five lists about a text ranging from top five reasons to read the book, top five favorite quotes, top five favorite moments, and so on. If students choose this option, it's important to emphasize that they must also include analysis and not just the lists.
- **Historical connections.** For this lens, students take a deeper dive into the historical backdrop of a piece of literature and discuss how the historical backdrop affects character, plot, and theme. Students can also explore what the theme shows or teaches about the cultural beliefs that surround the setting of the story.

3. **Produce the podcast.** After prepping the podcast episode script, students can move on to recording, producing, and editing their episode. They can also assign roles to determine who will be on air versus behind the scenes to produce clear audio quality and smooth pacing without any background noise or interruptions.

4. **Consider the technology.** Students do not need much in the way of equipment to record a quality podcast. Recording can even be done using the microphone on a smartphone, tablet, or laptop in a quiet room to help reduce background noise. As students record, I have the producer mark the time for anything that needs to be edited out such as a random car alarm going off in the distance or a dog

barking outside. That way, the producer can go back and edit out those sounds as needed. Free recording software such as Audacity works for both PCs and Macs. I recommend this program because it's user-friendly and has tons of capabilities for editing the episode, layering in music and sound effects, fading in and out, altering sound volume, and more. Mac users can also use GarageBand to do the same thing. Beyond these tech platforms, if a group of students has access to a higher-quality microphone, they can certainly use it, but, again, students do not need to go out and purchase any equipment to produce a quality podcast episode. To enhance their episodes with creativity and flair, students can use free sound libraries like `Freesound.org` to add sound effects and jingle music. There are other free music sites online that students can explore, but it's crucial that students understand and comply with copyright laws—especially if they plan to post their podcast episode anywhere online. Alternatively, students can write their own original music or create their own original sound effects for the episode, which adds a whole new level of creativity to the project. As students record and edit their episodes, they can use headphones to catch smaller issues and fine-tune the production so that the final product sounds as professional as possible. When they are ready, groups can submit a link to their podcasts to share with the class.

5. **Share and reflect.** The PodClassics Project concludes with a listening party when groups share their podcast episodes. Peer groups can then choose podcasts to listen to and provide constructive feedback, highlighting "roses and thorns" or "glows and grows" to identify each episode's strengths and areas for improvement. Students then reflect on their own podcast episode and think about what they have learned through the process of creating a podcast episode and how this project deepened their understanding of the literature. To extend the project, students could publish their podcasts on a class website to share with students, teachers, and

parents, or they could even design episode covers and logos. If other ELA teachers complete this same project at the same time, classes can even swap podcast episodes to assess. Additionally, teachers can offer extra credit for listening to additional episodes and filling out listening guides.

The PodClassics Project offers students a special opportunity to blend critical thinking, creativity, and collaboration while taking a deeper dive into a work of literature or real-world issue. By presenting analysis through a podcast, students learn additional audio production skills that are in demand in today's job market. This project also helps students practice skills such as organizing ideas, constructing arguments, analyzing ideas, communicating effectively, and working collaboratively. I especially appreciate that this project targets listening skills as students go back to review their peers' podcast episodes, which hones their ability to comprehend and process auditory information. Some states still include a listening component on graduation exams—for instance, the New York State Regents Exam features a listening section in its ELA portion. A podcast project offers an engaging way to help students strengthen these essential listening skills in a real-world context. Ultimately, this project can engage students in a nontraditional and creative way that will stick with them as they move through their educational careers.

Soundtrack Symposium

When I was completing my undergraduate degree, one of my British literature professors gave us the option of creating a soundtrack for a text that we studied during the semester course. At that point, I had never heard of such a project and was elated to have a creative option that involved music because I am passionate about music and like to write songs. To be handed the opportunity to use music as a lens for analyzing literature made complete sense because it enabled me to express my analysis through music that I loved, and that project became one of very few that I remember from my undergrad courses. It made an impact. This same engagement comes alive when I assign this project to my students. According to Goering and Strayhorn (2016), "Music can be used to teach English in ways that go beyond enhancement to deep integration, where music and English are taught together to deepen students' understanding of both subjects" (30). The project tasks students to prepare a soundtrack for a movie adaptation of the text or as a supplement to the reading experience itself—a carefully planned stop-and-listen plan that calls students to engage with specific pieces of music at key moments in the story.

Helpful Hint: Before assigning this project, provide a model by creating a listening list that accompanies a unit of study. For instance, create a list of songs or instrumental pieces for each chapter of a novel, and as students read each chapter, they can stop to listen to the songs and then discuss how the music connects to the reading. The text-to-text connection can be powerful in helping students increase the complexity of their analysis.

Although a powerful text can give us a powerful, emotional experience, so can music. Marrying the two together furthers the connection between our intellectual filter and emotional senses in such a powerful way. As we see top universities now offering courses that use Taylor Swift's music as a lens to study the literature and reflect on the world, we can see the power of connecting texts as a path to facilitate analysis. In fact, a soundtrack project can be a powerful, interdisciplinary assignment. Here's why:

- It enriches literary analysis skills through connecting songs or pieces of music that relate to characters, conflicts, emotions, tone, and more.
- It encourages creativity that allows for students to make connections between the text and songs they love—or even new music that students compose.
- It develops critical thinking skills through comparative analysis as students must justify and support the connections between the music and the literature.

- It increases student investment in learning because it taps into student interest, making the literature more relevant and relatable.
- It fosters interdisciplinary learning as the project integrates literature, music, and technology for a multitiered learning experience.
- It can also help students build empathy as they explore the emotional depths of the characters and their conflicts.

The objective of the Soundtrack Symposium assignment is to build a soundtrack for an assigned text and then present the soundtrack, focusing on making connections between the music and the literature backed by textual evidence. Here are the basic steps for the project and ways for students to share their musical connections:

1. **Select a work of literature and a focus.** To begin, students select a text for the soundtrack project and then begin to select pieces of music to pair with the text, making connections based on these criteria:
   - Themes
   - Characters
   - Plot points
   - Tones and moods
   - Conflicts
   - Chapters/sections

   To help students fully understand the power that music has to create an emotional connection, it's important for students to observe how music creates meaning.

2. **Make observations.** Next, students need to grasp the power that music must evoke to create emotion and communicate tone. To do this, show scenes from films where the musical piece or song plays particular importance in conveying the emotional depth of the moment. To do this, I like to play a movie clip silently first and ask students what the images convey in terms of character,

theme, setting, or conflict. Then, I play the movie clip again, this time with the sound turned on so that students can think consciously about how the music affects their interpretation of the scene. Here are a few movie scenes I like to use as an introduction to this project:

- The opening feather scene from *Forrest Gump*—Alan Silvestri's "Feather Theme" is an incredibly sweet and gentle piano piece that evokes nostalgia right at the beginning of the movie.
- A shark attack from the movie *Jaws*—John Williams brilliantly created an intense moment by using only two, iconic notes that foreshadow the trouble and tragedy of a shark attack.
- The scene from *Garden State* when Natalie Portman's character, Sam, gives her headphones to Zach Braff's character, Andrew Largeman, in the waiting room at a doctor's office—The Shins' beautifully angsty song "New Slang" plays over a shared set of headphones as the "meet-cute" for these two characters.
- The opening scene from my favorite Steven Spielberg film *Empire of the Sun*, where we see a ship running over coffins floating in the river juxtaposed with the music of a Welsh lullaby sung by Jamie, the protagonist, played by a young Christian Bale in his film debut. The song "Suo Gan" is one of the most beautiful pieces of choral music I've ever heard, and in the film, we hear young choir boys singing this peaceful lullaby alongside scenes of death to foreshadow the death of innocence that is to follow for young Jamie.

Students can discuss how the music affects or informs what we see on the screen. This exercise models what students are to do in the project—pair music or songs that reflect the emotionality of a situation in a text. Once students have a solid understanding of the impact music has on how we perceive the dynamics of scene, they can begin to work toward compiling their own soundtracks.

3. **Select songs and/or instrumental music.** Students get into their groups and research, analyze, and discuss various songs and/or pieces of music that relate to the text in a meaningful way. The number of songs for this project can vary greatly—from identifying a single song as a shorter, small-group class activity up to 12 songs to compile an entire soundtrack. For each song or piece of music, students write a justification that includes the song title and artist and an explanation for how the song connects to the text using textual evidence from both the song (as applicable) and the work of literature. Students should also take the sequence of the songs into careful consideration because they should track the chronology of the story in a logical and meaningful way, reflecting the overall arc of the story.

4. **Present the soundtrack.** After students have compiled the soundtrack for the piece of literature, it's time to design a presentation. Because this project could potentially involve up to 12 songs, it's important to think about how much time it would take for a group to present this much content. To account for time, I typically require that students present only four of the songs to the class; however, they still turn in their written analysis of all required songs. To present their songs to the class, students can use a slideshow presentation as a visual aid to explain the connections between the music and the text. I also require students to play a short clip (20–30 seconds) of any song that the class might not know. For instance, when a group presented on Remarque's novel *All Quiet on the Western Front,* they used an actual song from World War Two entitled "The White Cliffs of Dover" by Vera Lynn. Because this was a song the class did not know, the group played a 30-second clip to the class and then went into their explanation. Using a straightforward presentation approach like this works effectively, but there are other creative formats students can use. For example:

- Spotify playlist
- CD or record jacket

- Concert poster
- Interactive QR code playlist

Whichever format students choose to use, presentations should begin with a summary of the text and a brief biography of the author, followed by a track-by-track presentation of the soundtrack, including the reasons and evidence that explain the correlation. At the end of the presentation, students can include remarks about how connecting music to literature has affected their interpretation or understanding of the text. Alternatively, the presentation component can be more of a casual listening party in which each group plays one song from their soundtrack to the class accompanied by the explanation and analysis.

5. **Reflect on the project.** After sharing soundtracks, students should reflect on the learning journey of the project by answering essential questions such as:

   - What new understandings or insights did the project reveal about the text?
   - In what ways does music (or comparative literature) deepen comprehension of a story?
   - Why is it important to make text-to-text connections when we read?

Students can explore their answers to these questions individually, in small groups, or with the whole class to conclude the project.

The Soundtrack Symposium enables students to connect their love of music with literary analysis, and students typically get excited about being able to talk about the music they love. Music stirs emotions and can be such a powerful tool of comparative analysis that help students better relate to a story, making abstract ideas more approachable. Students remember this project because of the way it combines personal passion with literature. We can use this same concept when we teach literature and connect texts to songs that students know and love to build their appreciation for literature. For instance, try beginning a novel unit over *The Outsiders* with Taylor Swift's song "You Belong with Me" and see how it resonates with students.

Literary Cooking Show

Food. I can't think of a better way to engage teenagers than with food. Food has always played its part in storytelling either as something symbolic that points to theme, a means for revealing character traits, or even a mark of the cultural history of the setting. Think about the role food plays in these texts:

- *The Grapes of Wrath* by John Steinbeck—This is more of an obvious example of how food can symbolize theme as the grapes in the novel represent both the promise of prosperity and the bitter irony of the suffering they experience instead.
- *The Hunger Games* by Suzanne Collins—Bread becomes an important symbol of survival and hope but also defiance as shown when Peeta gives bread to Katniss.
- *Esperanza Rising* by Pam Muñoz Ryan—The guavas represent Esperanza's nostalgia for home as she flees Mexico but also symbolize the bittersweet reality of change.

Using food as an approach to literary interpretation offers a way to bring any text to life in a meaningful way. Thus, in the Literary Cooking Show Project, students merge literary analysis with cooking by creating an important dish based on a text they have read. This dish can either be one explicitly mentioned in the text (like in the previous examples), or it can be a new dish that somehow correlates to thematic meaning in the story. Students present their analysis while putting on a pretend cooking show. While teaching the class how to make the food, students explain why the dish is important in the text and use textual evidence to analyze how it symbolically communicates thematic meaning in the text. Here are the steps to follow:

1. **Introduce the concept.** To start the project, it's important to model the concept of using food as a means to analyze literature. It's important that students can connect food in a story to its symbolic meaning and think beyond the concrete level to the abstract level expected of literary analysis. I prefer to use movie examples where food plays a key role to reflect character development and theme. Here are a few film clips I like to show as examples:

   - *Matilda.* In the movie adaptation of Roald Dahl's novel, Miss Trunchbull forces Bruce Bogtrotter to eat a gigantic chocolate cake as a punishment for stealing. In this scene, the cake represents overindulgence but also cruelty and oppression at the hands of an abusive principal (Dahl 1988).

   - *Ratatouille.* This is the dish served to the finicky restaurant critic Anton Ego that prompts him to remember a special moment from his childhood, breaking down his critical exterior. This one dish reignites Anton's passion for food, marking the shift in his character from pessimism to friendliness. The shift in Anton's character helps to communicate one of the film's themes about embracing the simple pleasures of life and challenging societal expectations (Bird 2007).

   - **Harry Potter series.** Although this series contains several moments that contain foods, beverages, and candies, butterbeer makes an appearance several times. It's a beverage shared with friends, symbolizing unity and companionship. It also represents the importance of finding joy during the hard times and sticking together as a unit against the forces of evil (Rowling 1998).

   - *The Hunger Games.* This movie uses the stark contrast between the Capitol feasts and the starvation of the people living in the poorer districts to show the drastic inequality of the state.

Katniss realizes this inequality, and the disparity in food comes to represent both rebellion and survival (Collins 2008).

- *Charlie and the Chocolate Factory.* Each child that visits Wonka's factory has a different experience with the candy that brings out each child's weakness and overall lack of humility. However, Charlie's behavior contrasts with the behavior of the other children as he approaches the Wonka factory with kindness and humbleness, ultimately leading to his inheriting the chocolate factory. Through the children's different interactions with the candy, the candy comes to symbolize morality and appreciation (Dahl 1964).

Showing food-related scenes from well-known movies helps students understand the concept of food as a thematic symbol. It also helps students pay more attention to how stories can use food metaphorically to communicate key topics.

2. **Understand a cooking show structure.** Next, because students use the framework of a cooking show or demonstration as the format for their presentations, they should spend time watching cooking shows to understand how they are structured. Select shows that connect with secondary students such as Rosanna Pansino, creator of YouTube's *Nerdy Nummies* or episodes of *The Great British Baking Show*. The YouTube show *Binging with Babish* makes for another entertaining option as the host re-creates iconic dishes from TV shows and movies, and he provides hilarious commentary during his shows (Note: be sure to preview episodes before showing them for school appropriateness). As students watch cooking shows, they can observe that a cooking show usually has some sort of introduction to the dish, or thesis statement, for the demonstration. For this project, students do the same but also connect the dish to the theme of a text. Students may also notice that hosts may use a combination of direct explanations with voiceovers and on-screen text to point out ingredients or tips. Other shows might also use humor or personal anecdotes to make the

cooking demonstration more memorable. All shows then proceed through the steps to make the dish, ending with a conclusion in which the host serves or presents the dish for tasting. In essence, a cooking show has a beginning, middle, and end just like any other presentation.

Helpful Hint: Students can either create a filmed version of their cooking show or present it live in class. I prefer that students film it so that they can use a real kitchen instead of bringing in all the ingredients to school—some of which get left behind in my classroom. Gross! However, I have had students complete this project effectively both ways—recorded and live. Just make sure that students take all their food ingredients, tools, and items home on the day of the presentations. Trust me on this one.

3. **Select a text and write the script.** After students have been introduced to the concept of using food as a lens for literary analysis, they can select a work of literature that has food as an important, symbolic device. Students can then begin the process of writing the script for their food demonstration including their literary analysis. The script should include these elements:

   - An introduction to the text, author, and any relevant background information
   - A detailed description of the food or beverage that they are going to make
   - An explanation of how the dish connects to the text
   - Literary analysis that includes textual evidence and an explanation of how the food connects to theme

   After creating the script, students can take their scripts through peer revision and editing before beginning to rehearse for the presentation. The script portion of this project serves as another way for students to write literary analysis in a more creative format.

4. **Rehearse or film.** Once students have completed their scripts, it's time to rehearse for a live cooking demonstration or prepare for filming. Student presentations should be clearly organized and well-rehearsed to avoid any mishaps on the due date. Students need to have their food prepared in its different stages for the live cooking demonstration for the sake of time. For example, if students are going to make bread, there isn't enough time in class to wait for the bread to rise or to cook the bread in the oven. To work around the time challenge, students must practice and prepare the bread, in this case, at its different stages. This means they would need one that has already been mixed and shows the rising action as well as bread that has already been kneaded thoroughly and one that has been completely cooked. When students don't rehearse, it can cause massive time problems in the presentation. If students choose to film the cooking demonstration, they need to plan out the scenes to record, including closeups of anything such as ingredients or the final dish. For this option, students spend their time filming and editing instead of prepping for a live demonstration.

   Helpful Hint: Depending on the class and the resources available to students, an alternative to a live demonstration or filming could be a slideshow that depicts how to cook the dish using photographs alongside their analysis of the text. It's important to stay mindful of the student population and their ability to afford the supplies needed to complete a cooking project before assigning a project like this one.

5. **Assess the project.** On presentation day, students either share their cooking projects, showcase their cooking demonstrations, or share their slideshows along with the required analysis of the literature. Students are assessed on the quality of their literary analysis and how well they create a rich connection between the chosen dish and

the themes and characters of the text. They are also assessed on the clarity of their instructions and the organization of the presentation. As groups present, students can fill out a listening guide that holds them accountable for paying attention and for reflecting on the quality of the other presentations.

Helpful Hint: At the end of a presentation, students typically bring a sample of the dish to share out to students in class. Although students love this part of the project, be mindful of any student food allergies and give instructions about food preparation accordingly.

Overall, the Literary Cooking Show Project is one of the most engaging and effective ways for students to deepen their ability to analyze literature because it promotes critical thinking, creativity, and communication. Focusing on food as a symbolic lens enables students to understand themes of a text in a way that is tangible, meaningful, and fun. Any time students can have fun doing something creative for class, it makes the learning more memorable and inspires students to put more thought into their work. Because this project sees better student engagement, it can help build student confidence in giving presentations and being able to articulate complex ideas in a unique, relatable way, which is the goal in any classroom.

The Innovative ELA Teacher Pack

Don't forget to access the Innovative ELA Teacher Pack of 50 FREE and EXCLUSIVE resources through the following QR code. Simply follow the QR code over to the Bespoke ELA website to download all 50 FREE resources that accompany the assignments, lessons, activities, and projects found in this book.

Scan the QR code. Then use the password JaneAusten1775 to log in and download.

CHAPTER SIX

Innovative Research Projects

The days are well behind us when a research project simply meant writing a formulaic essay or putting lifeless ideas onto a poster board. Traditional research assignments set up students to regurgitate information, oftentimes without having to access deeper, more meaningful understandings and analysis. However, because students need to master the important skill of research, we need to revamp the topics and final products for the sake of student buy-in. By using more creative research topics with more innovative presentation formats, we can tap learners' innate curiosity and creativity, nurturing an environment in which all learners can thrive. This chapter explores creative ideas for research projects that can inspire deeper levels of student involvement and ownership of learning while increasing student skill development. Let's look at high-interest research project ideas that will engage learners through their mysterious or sensational content.

Unsolved Crime Investigation

Crime stories have captured our imaginations as shown by the sheer volume of crime podcasts, TV shows, and movies that now exist—all the result of popular demand. In this project, students become detectives who work to find evidence to solve a real-world crime. They are not necessarily going to go out in the field and interview witnesses or work

135

with law enforcement about an unsolved crime. Instead, students conduct research and put together the clues they find in the media representation of an unsolved case to put forth a thesis as to who they think committed a crime. In essence, learners become crime scene investigators via their research—like becoming armchair detectives (Dobbs 2019a).

1. **Research an unsolved crime.** For this project, it's important to keep in mind that students could possibly come across some disturbingly graphic content online such as crime scene photos. Therefore, before beginning the project, I like to give my students a list of unsolved crimes to choose from that have plenty of media coverage but involve crimes such as robberies, finances, fraud, or pirating to lessen their exposure to the disturbing content that comes along with murder cases (Dobbs 2019a). That being said, if a group wants to take on an unsolved murder case, I recommend discussing it with them and asking for parental permission before giving the green light. Here are some of the unsolved cases I usually recommend:

   - The Isabella Stewart Gardner Museum heist (1990)
   - The D. B. Cooper skyjacking (1971)
   - The Great Train Robbery (1963)
   - The Antwerp diamond heist (2003)
   - The Boston Brinks heist (1950)
   - The Baker Street Bank burglary (1971)

   There are many other cases like these to explore, but these have tons of information available via podcasts, TV shows, newspapers, magazines, interviews, documentaries, and movies—plenty of content for learners to use as research for the project while avoiding graphic material.

2. **Create a thesis and gather evidence.** After completing their research, students formulate a thesis statement about who they think committed the crime, backed by evidence found in the research. To do this,

students identify who is to blame for the crime based on what they find during the research process. This will become the central argument for the presentation.

3. **Present to the class.** Groups then present their findings to the class as a written report, a mock trial, a multimedia presentation, a podcast, or other means (Dobbs 2019a). The goal is to present convincing evidence that proves who committed the crime.

The Unsolved Crime Investigation Project engages student groups about research because it involves mystery and real-world crimes that need to be solved. One day, a group may discover that they were correct in their hypothesis. That's exciting!

Unveiling Conspiracy Theories

Conspiracy theories are another fascinating topic to explore. In this project, student groups conduct research to discover how and why conspiracy theories exist, focusing on the following research questions:

- What function or purpose do conspiracy theories fulfill?
- What is a famous conspiracy theory that gives an example of why they exist?

1. **Research conspiracy theories.** Students research the psychological, cultural, and historic reasons people create or support conspiracy theories. To begin this project, consider exploring iconic conspiracy theories such as the following:
    - The 1969 faking of the moon landing
    - The person, persons, or groups who conspired to assassinate President John F. Kennedy
    - The hidden evidence of extraterrestrial life at Area 51

    As groups conduct their research, they will come across many more conspiracy theories to explore for this project. Like most people, students find conspiracy theories fascinating, but what makes them so interesting? The research shows that people invent conspiracy theories to fulfill a need for answers to things we do not know or understand. The unknown presents a scary and unpredictable world that can cause anxiety and fear. These are the very concepts that students explore throughout the project.

2. **Create a website.** By designing a website, learners gain hands-on experience with web design, a marketable skill in our present-day world, along with necessary ELA skills such as conducting research, organizing ideas, and presenting findings via a digital platform.

For the website itself, learners can use a template from Canva or any other web-building program of choice such as Google Sites, Wix, or Weebly. The website should include the following pages:

- **Home page.** Gives an overview of the website and its purpose to inform the public about conspiracy theories
- **Analysis page.** Answers the research questions backed by credible sources
- **Conspiracy theory profile page.** Presents the case of a conspiracy theory along with specific information about its origin and cultural impact
- **Debunking page.** Shares evidence that refutes conspiracy theories in general and disproves the specific one profiled on the website
- **Interactive page.** Gives a quiz or presents an infographic on key points from the website

3. **Present research findings.** After groups have finished creating their websites, they can present their websites to the class along with their research findings. Students like this project because it fosters curiosity about mysteries. By investigating how and why people create conspiracy theories, students learn to become healthy skeptics by questioning what they read, analyzing evidence, and evaluating the power of media.

Infamous Criminal Case Notebook Project

Researching an infamous criminal can be far more captivating than researching traditional ELA topics such as school uniforms, homework, and college tuition, which tend to fall flat because they have been so overused. Students tend to select topics like these because they think teachers want to hear these ideas from them in a research project. They like to play it safe instead of selecting a topic that truly interests them. Because these are such overused topics, they tend to lead to shallow analysis with little originality and can feel like a chore instead of a passion project. Shifting the focus to an infamous criminal can motivate learners because the material itself is more captivating. For this project, students research a famous criminal and build a detailed case notebook that investigates the crime, the investigation, and the media coverage of the case. However, the project goes beyond just telling the criminal's story. It asks learners to evaluate sources, synthesize material, and draw conclusions about the bigger issues that could have led the criminal to a life of crime and the impact that media has on the public's perception of a suspect (Dobbs 2019a).

> *Helpful Hint*: Consider giving groups a list of approved criminals (sounds ironic!). Similar to the Unsolved Crime Investigation Project, be mindful of the content that students might see when researching an infamous criminal. I tend to leave out serial killers and terrorists from this project because of the graphic nature of photos available online. Please use your own discretion here.

1. **Select a criminal to research.** Students begin by conducting preliminary research to select a criminal to research. The following list contains options for infamous criminals with fascinating life stories (and crimes) to use for this project:

    - Bernie Madoff
    - Frank Abagnale, Jr.

- Anna Delvey
- Bonnie and Clyde
- Doris Payne
- Charles Ponzi
- Harvey "Machine Gun" Kelly
- Al Capone
- The "Barefoot Bandit," Colton Harris-Moore
- Mark Hofmann
- Ronnie Biggs
- Patricia Hearst
- Martha Stewart
- Abby Lee Miller
- The Anglin Brothers
- Victor Lustig
- Benedict and Margaret Arnold
- Elizabeth Holmes

There are many more criminals to choose from for this project, and a student can even find their own criminal to research with teacher approval. These figures and their crimes provide an excellent backdrop for analyzing human behavior, societal issues, and similar tragic flaws that we see reflected in literature: ambition, greed, and *hubris*.

2. **Research the criminals and create a case notebook.** Students then move on to creating a case notebook that contains three sections:
    - Section 1: The criminal's life and crime(s)
    - Section 2: Media source analysis
    - Section 3: Synthesis and conclusions

To get started, students gather information for their case notebook from various sources, including books, news articles, documentaries, interviews, court transcripts, police reports, eyewitness accounts, and expert commentary. Their research focuses at first on the details of the criminal's life and crimes, detailing what happened, the investigation, and the trial. Students compile their findings about the criminal's life of crime in Section 1 of the notebook. They can be creative with how they present information in this section and re-create records, letters, and photographs to bring the criminals' story to life.

Throughout the research process, they also must evaluate how the media depicted the case and assess media sources for potential bias. They compile this analysis in Section 2 of the notebook. In this section, students include annotated resources along with a source analysis form to critically evaluate the key materials used in their project.

Section 3 requires students to craft a written reflection that synthesizes their research and draws conclusions about their findings. For this section, they can reflect on the following questions:

- What significant life events or circumstances might have led the criminal to a path of crime?
- What factors contributed to the criminal's choices to turn to a life of crime?
- Were there any moments in the criminal's life when a potential intervention or opportunity could have changed the criminal's life path?
- Did the criminal act out of greed, ambition, urgent need, or something else? How do you know?
- What role, if any, did mental health, addiction, or other personal struggles play in their crimes?
- What does this case reveal about the values, fears, or biases of the society in which it occurred?

- How did the media shape public perception of the criminal?
- How did the criminal's actions affect other people, and what does this show about the consequences of crime?
- How was the criminal punished? Did the punishment fit the crime? Do you agree or disagree with the punishment the criminal received? Why or why not?
- What can we learn about crime prevention from this criminal's case?
- Was there a systemic failure involved that made it easier for the criminal to commit the crime?
- What does this case reveal about human nature and morality?
- What can we learn from this case about how we can approach crime rehabilitation today?

3. **Share the case notebook with the class.** After compiling the case notebook, groups can share them with the class followed by a discussion about what we can learn by studying the lives of criminals. The Infamous Criminal Case Notebook Project offers an in-depth study into the legal, social, and psychological aspects of criminals. It enables students to conduct research and analysis on an intriguing topic to synthesize information about the complexity of criminals' lives and the role of the justice system. By targeting skills needed to conduct research, analyze sources, and synthesize findings, this project can help to motivate intellectual curiosity. Once students know they can go beyond the commonplace topics to something as unexpected as a criminal's life of crime, they can find passion and inspiration to see the project through to the end.

Star-Crossed Lovers Project

Star-crossed lovers have always captured our hearts and continue to do so. Love is an incredibly powerful force—to the point that it's addictive—so when two lovers can't be together, it seems catastrophic (Dobbs 2023a). For this project, learners aim to define the traits of star-crossed love stories through literature, film, music, history, podcasts, TED Talks, and psychology, culminating in the creation of an anthology that analyzes the key themes of the genre. For the final piece of the anthology, students write an original star-crossed love story that showcases the traits they have discovered and then reflect on how their anthologies shed new light about the genre.

I typically assign this project after we study a core text that involves star-crossed lovers such as *Romeo and Juliet*, *The Great Gatsby*, *The Love Suicides at Amijima*, *Wuthering Heights*, or sections from Ovid's *Metamorphosis* like the stories of "Pyramus and Thisbe," "Orpheus and Eurydice," "Apollo and Daphne," "Cephalus and Procris," and "Venus and Adonis." Starting the project with a whole-class literary unit helps prepare them for the group work ahead and helps them begin to generate a list of traits for their anthology projects (Dobbs 2023a). For example, traits of star-crossed love stories that come through *Romeo and Juliet* include the conflict of fate and desire, impulsive actions, family pressure, and tragic sacrifice. Students continue adding traits to this starter list throughout the project to evidence an understanding of how they work to create dramatic tension and *catharsis*.

This project requires that students include and analyze one work of literature, one song, one film, one real-life story from history, one podcast or TED Talk, and finally, create an original story. Here are a few sources to consider as options:

- **Literature**
    - "Annabel Lee" by Edgar Allan Poe
    - "My Last Duchess" by Robert Browning
    - "La Belle Dame sans Merci" by John Keats
    - "Interpreter of Maladies" by Jhumpa Lahiri

- **Songs**
    - "Fortnight" by Taylor Swift
    - "Love Story" by Taylor Swift

- "The Scientist" by Coldplay
- "Travelin' Soldier" by The Chicks
- "Ho Hey" by The Lumineers

- **Films**
  - *Edward Scissorhands*
  - *Phantom of the Opera*
  - *West Side Story*
  - *Titanic*
  - *The Fault in Our Stars*
  - *La La Land*
  - *A Walk to Remember*

- **Real-Life Stories from History**
  - Cleopatra and Mark Antony
  - Tristan and Isolde
  - Napoleon and Josephine
  - Richard Burton and Elizabeth Taylor
  - Bonnie and Clyde

- **Podcasts and TED Talks**
  - "Star-Crossed Lovers" from *Shelf-Involved*
  - "How Dopamine Drives Love, Creativity & Addiction w/Daniel Z. Lieberman, MD EP 1255" from *The School of Greatness*
  - "The Brain in Love" by Helen Fisher (TED Talk)
  - "The Science of Falling in Love" by Shannon Odell (TED-ed)

- **Articles**
  - "From Star-Crossed Lovers to Forbidden Love—Why we Always Want What We Can't Have" by Ariane Resnick, CNC for *Very Well Mind*
  - "Love and the Brain" by Richard Schwartz and Jacqueline Olds for *Harvard Medical School*
  - "The Psychology of Love: 10 Groundbreaking Insights into the Science of Relationships" by Eric W. Dolan for *PsyPost*

1. **Research star-crossed lovers.** To begin the project, students complete the star-crossed lovers analysis chart for each required component, which involves a summary of the text, a list of traits, key quotations, and a theme statement that comes through the text.

   As students compile their list of traits, they essentially answer the question, "What are the defining traits of star-crossed love stories?" The following list contains examples of these traits:

   - Forbidden love
   - Unrequited love
   - Feuds
   - War
   - Class differences
   - Intense passion
   - Sacrificing family and friends
   - Tragic misunderstandings
   - Confidantes
   - Societal pressure
   - Supernatural forces
   - Prejudice
   - Separation
   - Death
   - Suicide
   - Reconciliation

2. **Compile the research.** Using their research, students write a short story or create a notebook (physical or online) about a new pair of star-crossed lovers that reflect their understanding of the genre.

`BookCreator.com` or Canva can help students create an online version of their research. Again, there are several ways to modify this assignment to fit student needs, such as giving them the resources to use or shortening the scope of requirements. In the end, students learn to appreciate a genre that has influenced the world for thousands of years and will continue to do so far into the future. But why? That's precisely what students aim to discover through this project. Whether through the poetic lines of *Romeo and Juliet* or the doomed setting of the *Titanic*, star-crossed love stories reveal our need for connection despite the barriers that may separate us (Dobbs 2023a).

Paranormal Investigative Zine

First off, a "zine" is short for magazine and these are small, self-published booklets that can be published on a low budget in limited quantities. In many ways, the trademark of a zine is its do-it-yourself aesthetic. Students can create a handmade zine with a collage-style layout and hand-drawn artwork with unique fonts, stapled into a booklet to achieve a personalized feel. They can even create a zine that's more like a "junk journal," a booklet made from "junk"—including napkins, scrapbook paper, stickers, envelopes, stamps, buttons, cutouts, and anything else the creator would like to include (Dobbs 2021). See Figures 6.1–6.3 for examples from a junk journal zine about Jane Austen's novel *Sense and Sensibility*. Because zines can be about anything from personal stories to politics, we can adapt this format in secondary ELA to house any sort of project and any type of writing assignment. Although I prefer for students to handmake their zines, they can also create them online if preferable.

For this project, learners become investigative journalists about a paranormal phenomenon in the world and use the zine as the format to compile and present their research. They are charged with exploring the paranormal world through conducting research, writing fascinating articles, and creating visual displays. In addition, students also practice

FIGURE 6.1 Junk journal zine: Jane Austen's *Sense and Sensibility*.

critical thinking as they work to discern fact from fiction while they practice the key ELA skills of research, analysis, and news writing.

1. **Choose and research paranormal topics.** To get started, students get into groups and select a paranormal topic that interests them, or they can conduct initial research to find their own paranormal topic of interest. Students find the following list of paranormal topics interesting:

   - Haunted locations
   - UFO sightings
   - Shadow people

- Bigfoot/Sasquatch
- The Loch Ness monster
- Skinwalker Ranch
- The Bermuda Triangle
- Area 51
- King Tut's cursed tomb
- Crop circles
- Marfa lights
- Crying or bleeding statues
- Kraken

FIGURE 6.2 Junk journal zine: Most important word in *Sense and Sensibility*.

Innovative Research Projects   **149**

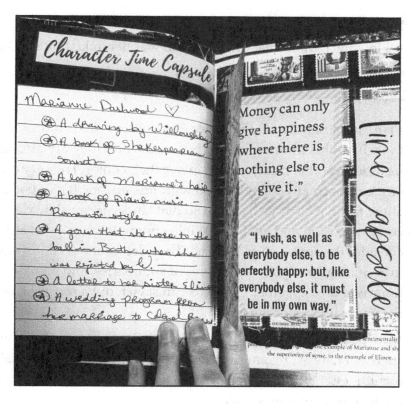

FIGURE 6.3 Junk journal zine: Time capsule page for *Sense and Sensibility*.

Once students have made their topic selection, they can begin the research process by exploring newspaper and magazine articles, documentaries, podcasts, books, and any other relevant media to gather information for the content of their zine. The zine should include the following:

- A creative title
- The origin story of the phenomenon
- Key witnesses and interview quotes
- Historical background of the phenomenon
- Catalog of evidence

- Poetry or fan fiction piece(s)
- How the paranormal phenomenon was debunked (if applicable)
- Art, graphics, and photos that are relevant to the topic
- Works cited

2. **Plan the structure of the zine.** Students are free to decide how to include this information in their zines, and they are also free to include any other creative elements of their choice. The very essence of a zine is creative freedom, so with this project, it's important to allow for that creative freedom so that students can showcase their comprehension and analysis. While aiming for creativity, students consider the structure of the zine. They determine sections, such as introduction, analysis, reflections, or summaries, and plan how sections will flow together. Students can sketch out a rough layout for the pages like a storyboard.

3. **Incorporate text and analysis.** Students integrate written content, such as analysis, responses to key questions, or summaries. They include evidence and examples to support points, whether from the text or their own research.

4. **Add creative elements.** Visuals, collages, hand-drawn illustrations, or cut-out photos are used to express thoughts. The zine remains visually engaging while clearly communicating analysis.

5. **Format and organize the zine.** Students organize and format their zine for visual appeal. They experiment with different layouts, fonts, and colors, ensuring the design complements the content and makes it easy for readers to follow the ideas.

6. **Revise and edit.** After completing the first draft, students revisit their zine. They check for errors in grammar, analysis, and MLA formatting. Creative elements are evaluated to ensure they support the message without overwhelming the content.

7. **Finalize and present.** Once satisfied, students finalize their pages and prepare to share with the class. They present their zine verbally,

explaining their choices and how creative elements tie into their analysis. They can also pass them around the room for students to explore on their own.

Stephen Merrill and Sarah Gonser (2023) state, "When students get to make decisions about their learning, it can be powerfully motivating." When they have this kind of freedom, they can personalize their learning and express their ideas in a more meaningful way. By giving students some autonomy over their work, they are more likely to take more ownership of their learning, which tends to increase motivation and mindset.

In the Paranormal Investigative Zine Project, students are tasked with integrating creativity, research, and critical thinking by taking on the persona of an investigative journalist. By exploring paranormal phenomena, students can enjoy the mystery that surrounds these fascinating topics while practicing important skills. Giving students more agency in their own learning can develop a greater appreciation for the investigative process.

Who's to Blame? Disaster Research Project

This project concept was inspired by my own personal fascination with the Donner Party disaster of 1846–1847 in which a group of travelers became trapped in the Sierra Nevada Mountains by heavy snowfall in November 1846. The first help couldn't reach them until February 1847, and in the meantime, many members of the party succumbed to starvation and freezing temperatures. When their food supplies ran out, the group reportedly turned to cannibalism to survive. Of the 86 original members of the party, only 46 survived. But what happened? Who's to blame for these deaths?

Through ample research, I concluded that there were two primary factors in the Donner Party tragedy: leaving one month too late in the spring to avoid the heavy snowfall and following a reported (but unsubstantiated) shortcut published in a guidebook. My fascination about this incident led me to create The Donner Party Nonfiction Unit (for sale in the Bespoke ELA Teachers Pay Teachers shop). This project concept provided the impetus for students to explore other disasters, leading to the guiding question, "Who's to blame?"

Disasters can be human-made, or they can come from nature. Many disasters from history have been caused from a combination of human decisions, situations outside human control (such as weather), and overall lack of planning or organization to deal with the fallout from the disaster. For this project, students select a disaster that interests them and conduct research to evaluate who is to blame for what happened and who should be held accountable for the outcome. In essence, this project acts like an argumentative essay. Students synthesize their findings from their research to present a convincing case to the class about the person or persons responsible for a famous disaster.

1. **Select a disaster.** The first step in this project involves selecting a disaster from history. Students can complete initial research to discover a tragic story that sparks their interest. To get started, here is a list of disasters that students tend to find intriguing:

    - The 1912 sinking of *RMS Titanic*
    - The 2004 Indian Ocean tsunami
    - Hurricane Katrina in 2005
    - The 1871 Great Chicago Fire
    - The 1986 Chernobyl accident
    - The 2011 Fukushima nuclear disaster
    - The 1937 Hindenburg explosion
    - The 1986 space shuttle *Challenger* disaster
    - The 1978 Jonestown massacre
    - The 1952 London smog
    - The 1906 San Francisco earthquake
    - The 2014 disappearance of Malaysia Airlines Flight 370

Students can use this list as a starting place, but they should focus on finding a disaster that interests and inspires them because their interest provides the motivation it takes to complete a quality project and present a convincing argument to the class.

2. **Research the disaster.** Next, students research the disaster, using credible resources to answer key questions about what occurred. Students should focus on the following:

   - **The cause.** What caused the disaster? Was it human error, bad luck, or natural forces?
   - **The key decisions.** What decisions led to the disaster, and who made them? Were these decisions influenced by misinformation, pride, and/or poor planning?
   - **The aftermath.** How did the people involved respond to the disaster? Do you agree or disagree with how things were handled after-the-fact? What were the immediate and long-term consequences of the disaster?
   - **The blame.** Consider all aspects that contributed to the disaster. Was anyone or any group at fault? Could there have been better preparation for the disaster? If there was an investigation after the disaster, do you agree or disagree with the findings? Essentially, who or what is to blame for the disaster?
   - **Analyzing the disaster.** What role did individuals, groups, or governments play in preventing or worsening the disaster? Could the disaster have been avoided? If so, how?
   - **Reflection.** How do the lessons from this disaster apply to today? What can we learn from this disaster to prevent something else like it from occurring in the future? What did you learn from researching this event?

3. **Present the research.** After students have completed their research to answer the key research questions, they present their case to the class. Just like an attorney must present a case to the jury, students

take on the role of convincing the class that their conclusions are sound, logical, and correct based on the evidence. Groups end their presentations with the question, "Did we convince you?" The students in the classroom act as a jury and vote yes or no. To ensure that students actively listen to group presentations, they should take notes along the way to help them arrive at their final votes.

The Who's to Blame? Disaster Research Project uses research to target critical analysis and showcase how students think through a problem as well as synthesize evidence into an evidence-based conclusion. Students build on important skills through peer analysis by giving and receiving feedback. The voting process encourages students to justify their decisions, pose thought-provoking questions, and build a community of intellectual curiosity. Accordingly, this project helps students learn how to communicate their ideas effectively and persuasively and reflect on historical disasters to prevent or better prepare for disasters in the future.

The Making of a Murderer Project

This project may sound like another criminal, nonfiction project; however, it focuses on using literature to analyze the factors that contribute to the making of a murderer. Students often ask me why "great" literature is so sad and contains so much death, and it's a great question to ask. Tragedies in life cause us the most growing pains in terms of overcoming the hardship involved, more so than the happy times in life. Art gives people a means to express and process hard times so that we can demystify the pain and suffering to cope with living.

The Making of a Murderer Project frames literary study with a psychological lens that delves into the depths of how and why someone could be driven to commit murder, which provides a more fascinating way to approach literature than through traditional lenses. This project explores how classic literature represents the motives, psychological behaviors, and circumstances that surround murders. Students investigate the circumstances within each text that drive a character to commit murder, allowing them to analyze themes centered on moral ambiguity, societal pressures, psychic trauma, and the human condition.

By close reading poems, short stories, novels, films, and plays that involve murder, students analyze the factors that made the murderer rethink the nature of justice, morality, and free will.

1. **Choose the text.** The following list contains texts to consider using for this project, separated into categories that represent the motivating force behind the murder(s) in each story. Please note that the way I've categorized these texts is open to debate, but these lists give a starting place for the unit.

   - **Murder for Power**
     - *Macbeth* by William Shakespeare
     - *Crime and Punishment* by Fyodor Dostoevsky
     - "My Last Duchess" by Robert Browning
     - "Porphyria's Lover" by Robert Browning
     - "Diary of a Madman" by Guy de Maupassant
     - *Animal Farm* by George Orwell
     - *Julius Caesar* by William Shakespeare
     - *The Hunger Games* by Suzanne Collins
     - *Faust* by Johann Wolfgang von Goethe

   - **Murder as the Result of Rejection**
     - *Frankenstein* by Mary Shelley
     - *Grendel* by John Gardner
     - "The Outcasts of Poker Flat" by Bret Harte
     - *The Outsiders* by S. E. Hinton
     - *Edward Scissorhands* by Tim Burton
     - *The Metamorphosis* by Franz Kafka

   - **Murder Due to Self-Defense**
     - *Fahrenheit 451* by Ray Bradbury
     - "The Most Dangerous Game" by Richard Connell

- *To Kill a Mockingbird* by Harper Lee
- *The Road* by Cormac McCarthy
- *The Crucible* by Arthur Miller
- *Beowulf*

- **Murder Based on Star-Crossed Lovers**
  - *Romeo and Juliet* by William Shakespeare
  - *The Love Suicides at Amijima* by Chikamatsu Monzaemon
  - *The Phantom of the Opera* by Andrew Lloyd Webber
  - *Wuthering Heights* by Emily Brontë
  - *The Great Gatsby* by F. Scott Fitzgerald
  - "The Highwayman" by Alfred Noyes
  - *West Side Story* by Jerome Robbins
  - "Pyramus and Thisbe" by Ovid

- **Murder Based on Revenge**
  - *Chronicle of a Death Foretold* by Gabriel Garcia Márquez
  - *Othello* by William Shakespeare
  - *Medea* by Euripides
  - "The Cask of Amontillado" by Edgar Allan Poe
  - *Oedipus the King* by Sophocles

- **Murder as the Result of Innate Evil**
  - *Lord of the Flies* by William Golding
  - *Heart of Darkness* by Joseph Conrad
  - *Dr. Jekyll and Mr. Hyde* by Robert Louis Stevenson

- **Murder as a Result of Racism**
  - *Cry, the Beloved Country* by Alan Paton
  - "The Moment the Gun Went Off" by Nadine Gordimer
  - "Desiree's Baby" by Kate Chopin
  - *The Hate U Give* by Angie Thomas
  - "Strange Fruit" by Abel Meeropol
  - "If We Must Die" by Claude McKay

- "Incident" by Countee Cullen
- *Just Mercy* by Bryan Stevenson
- *Twelve Years a Slave* by Solomon Northup

- **Murder That Occurs Because of Tradition**
  - "The Lottery" by Shirley Jackson
  - "2BO2B" by Kurt Vonnegut
  - "The Fall of the House of Usher" by Edgar Allan Poe
  - "The Ones Who Walk Away from Omelas" by Ursula K. Le Guin
  - *Things Fall Apart* by Chinua Achebe
  - *The Giver* by Lois Lowry
  - *Brave New World* by Aldous Huxley

- **Murder Based on War and Genocide**
  - *An Ordinary Man* by Paul Rusesabagina
  - "Rwanda: Where Tears Have No Power" by Haki R. Madhubuti
  - *Night* by Elie Wiesel
  - "The Charge of the Light Brigade" by Alfred Lord Tennyson
  - "The Sniper" by Liam O'Flaherty
  - *The Things They Carried* by Tim O'Brien
  - *All Quiet on the Western Front* by Erich Maria Remarque
  - "Dulce et Decorum Est" by Wilfred Owen
  - "I Have No Gun but I Can Spit" by Mahmoud Darwish
  - *Hotel Rwanda* by Terry George
  - *The Boy in the Striped Pajamas* by John Boyne
  - *Life Is Beautiful* by Robert Benigni and Vincenzo Cerami
  - Miklos Radnoti poems

- **Murder Based on Other Crimes Such as Robbery**
  - "In a Grove" by Ryūnosuke Akutagawa
  - "The Landlady" by Roald Dahl
  - *Oliver Twist* by Charles Dickens
  - *Treasure Island* by Robert Louis Stevenson
  - *A View from the Bridge* by Arthur Miller

- *The Dark Knight* by Christopher Nolan
- *The Outsiders* by S. E. Hinton

- **Murder as a Result of Paranoia and Insanity**
  - "A Tell-Tale Heart" by Edgar Allan Poe
  - "Lamb to the Slaughter" by Roald Dahl
  - *Of Mice and Men* by John Steinbeck

- **Murder as a Result of Scientific Experimentation**
  - *Never Let Me Go* by Kazuo Ishiguro
  - "The Birthmark" by Nathaniel Hawthorne
  - *The Twilight Zone:* "Eye of the Beholder"
  - "The Veldt" by Ray Bradbury
  - *Jurassic Park* by Michael Crichton
  - *The Island of Dr. Moreau* by H.G. Wells
  - *Flowers for Algernon* by Daniel Keyes

- **Murder Based on an Existential Crisis**
  - *Hamlet* by William Shakespeare
  - *I, Robot* by Alex Proyas
  - *The Stranger* by Albert Camus
  - *The Matrix* by Lana and Lilly Wachowski

- **Murder That Occurs Because of Civil Disobedience**
  - *Antigone* by Sophocles
  - "Harrison Bergeron" by Kurt Vonnegut
  - *The Book Thief* by Markus Zusak
  - *Selma* by Ava DuVernay

Students can either select texts from this list to explore, or they can be assigned a whole class text for close reading/viewing and analysis.

2. **Create an analysis chart.** As students read and analyze each text, they complete an analysis chart that requires them to categorize the

factors that cause the character(s) in the story to commit murder. In this project, students delve deeper into considering character development, conflicts, and themes in literature that involve murder in some capacity. Students analyze the motivations and justifications of fictional murderers to understand how and why murders occurs in real life. After all, literature mimics life and has so much to teach us when we lean in and listen.

Ultimately, students answer the focused research question—"Who or what drives a person to commit murder?"—by creating psychological profiles for three different characters who represent three different reasons as to what motivates people to kill another human being.

Through this process, students analyze the character's motivations, background, and cultural or situational influences that lead them to murder.

3. **Create a case file.** Through their analysis, students develop a comprehensive case file that responds to the focus question and synthesizes their findings into the top three reasons their selected characters committed murder, supported by textual evidence.

    Creative elements for the case file consist of, but are not limited to the following:

    - A police report summary of events
    - Illustrations or timelines of key events
    - Excerpts from interviews or letters written in the character's voice
    - Confession letters or tapes

4. **Present findings.** This creative portion of the project offers several presentation options, allowing students to choose the format that best suits their strengths and interests. Each format combines analytical rigor with creative expression, ensuring a

captivating and insightful final product. Students can choose from the following options:

- **Physical case file.** Students create a detailed dossier with notes, photographs, evidence, and analysis, replicating the format of a real investigation file.
- **Digital slideshow.** Students design a presentation featuring visuals, charts, and bullet points to highlight key aspects of the case and relevant themes.
- **Documentary-style video.** Students produce a video with voiceovers, dramatic reenactments, interviews, and background music to present the case dynamically.
- **Multimedia presentation.** Students combine visuals, text, and audio to engage the audience while exploring themes like moral ambiguity, psychological trauma, and societal influence.

These formats ensure students present both analytical insights and creative elements to captivate the audience.

Helpful Hint: As an extension to this project, students can make connections between the literary characters and real-life people who were motivated to commit murder based on similar reasons. For instance, a student might draw a parallel between Macbeth and King Henry VIII, who were both motivated by power to commit atrocities against their own people for the sake of power. This aspect of the project can also easily turn into a whole-class discussion over the topic.

In the end, The Making of a Murderer Project uses literature as the lens to analyze and attempt to understand the motivations that cause murder. Through analyzing fictional characters and their actions we can discover insights into psychological, social, and situational factors that can drive people to the most extreme acts possible. Literature offers a safe arena to explore these dark aspects of human nature. Students also learn to recognize the larger implications of these motives within and outside the realm of fiction to see how literature can teach us about the complexities of the human condition.

The Innovative ELA Teacher Pack

Don't forget to access the Innovative ELA Teacher Pack of 50 FREE and EXCLUSIVE resources through the following QR code. Simply follow the QR code over to the Bespoke ELA website to download all 50 FREE resources that accompany the assignments, lessons, activities, and projects found in this book.

Scan the QR code.
Then use the password
JaneAusten1775
to log in and download.

CHAPTER SEVEN

Innovative Strategies to Gamify the Classroom

Gamification within the classroom and in learning and development at the corporate level has become a popular method for students to acquire skills and a viable alternative to traditional teaching methods, which can fail to engage a diverse pool of learners. In the business world, many companies have turned to gamification with impressive results. For instance, Google announced that 100% of its employees submitted their travel expenses as a direct result of a gamification of their platform (Cornerstone 2024). Another company called Engine Yard, a cloud app management platform, gamified its system to encourage more employees to complete customer surveys and fix bugs in the system. As a result, they saw a 20% reduction in customer complaint tickets and a 40% increase in customer support response time (Cornerstone 2024). The fundamental learning and development tools are the same whether it's in the corporate world or in the classroom. By integrating tools to gamify learning experiences, students have more fun. Learning becomes more enjoyable and because of that emotional response, combined with the spirit of friendly competition, students are more likely to engage with the content with positive results. In this chapter, we will explore creative ways to gamify the English Language Arts (ELA) classroom through practical applications, tools, and insights that are affordable and possible to integrate into any curriculum.

But what are the fundamentals of gamifying learning? In essence, gamification involves using points, badges, leaderboards, and quests as incentives to drive interest in ELA content. Research shows a correlation between gamification and an increase in intrinsic motivation, a key driver in long-term academic success (Deterding et al. 2011). For example, by embedding a quest story into a lesson plan, students can develop an emotional connection to the content because of the purpose to complete, or win, the quest challenge. This is a useful tool in the ELA classroom as we continually battle against lack of interest and motivation. Students are already playing games on their own time, so by appealing to their personal interests, we can see better performance in the acquisition of important skills much like how many corporations are seeing this work for employees within their own learning and development platforms.

Some ways we can integrate gamification into secondary ELA include using RPGs (role-playing games) or quest-based challenges. To do this, students can take on the roles of characters from novels and complete challenges specific to that character to earn badges or team prizes. Such activities promote deeper comprehension and analysis while making the learning experience more memorable (Sheldon 2012). Platforms such as classcraft and Kahoot make it easy to implement game elements into lessons while giving teachers the flexibility to alter gaming elements as needed based on student performance (Kapp 2012).

Gamification also works great for differentiation because it can engage reluctant learners by making the learning experience interactive and more fun. For example, students who struggle with the writing process can move through learning module challenges based on writing skills, earning points and receiving frequent feedback that can keep them engaged more so than traditional assignments. More advanced students can use gamification to make predictions about the story or write alternate endings to classic works of literature.

However, it's important to keep in mind that the gamified elements are still connected to learning objectives to avoid the trap of just providing amusement without any meaningful educational reasons behind using them (Kapp 2012). This means striking a balance between fun and rigor, ensuring that the gamified elements add depth to a lesson and don't become a side distraction. The following sections detail practical ideas and resources to add gamified elements into ELA curriculum to help provide students with the motivation and engagement they need to acquire new skills for life.

Quest-Based Learning Adventures

There is something inherent within us that loves a great adventure. We love the suspense, the thrill, and the challenge involved in the journey to complete a quest. Think about the video games, movies, and stories based on the concept of a quest. It's archetypal. Because of our inherent interest to go on adventure quests, we can use quest-based learning adventures as an effective instructional strategy. This means integrating game-like elements with narrative structures and interactive challenges into a lesson to guide students through a learning experience. Essentially, students embark upon missions or quests to solve a problem, complete a task, or collaborate on a challenge activity. These quests align with specific learning objectives that involve the application of skills in a more interesting way than a regular worksheet activity. Quest-based learning has the power to motivate students to complete work more thoroughly and creatively. Through the educational content embedded within the quest narrative, learners become more active in the learning process instead of being a passive listener (Deterding et al. 2011).

But how are quest-based learning activities structured? Here's a basic framework:

- **Active Learning Through Storytelling**
  - Most quests use a narrative structure that engages the learner in practicing skills while moving along the journey to acquire the object of the quest (e.g., the stone from *Indiana Jones and the Temple of Doom*, Princess Peach from *Super Mario Brothers*, etc.).

- The narrative provides an interesting purpose for the activity that offers more engagement than a traditional, passive lesson (Sheldon 2012).

- **Incremental Challenges to Master Skills**
  - There are different ways to sequence challenges. One way is to have student groups complete tasks organized by increasing complexity. Another way is to organize the challenges by type of skill or by applying skills to new situations or contexts (Kapp 2012).
  - In an ELA classroom, for example, a quest might begin with identifying themes in different passages before having students write a theme of their own.

- **The Motivation Factor**
  - The mystery of motivation is still a mystery. There's never a guarantee that anything we do as teachers is going to motivate every single student sitting in our classrooms. However, when students can have fun while learning, there is a better chance that more students will participate.
  - Parents and educators alike debate how external rewards affect intrinsic motivation, and I'm not entering that debate here in this book. However, incorporating elements such as badges, points, and leaderboards into a quest can appeal to intrinsic motivation to master a skill while simultaneously using the extrinsic motivation of recognition and friendly competition to engage students in the learning process (Deterding et al. 2011).

- **Text Adventure Games with ChatGPT**
  - Radoff (2022) gives a quick-start way to use AI for building text-based adventure games. He also includes the following prompt to put into ChatGPT:

    > "I want you to act as if you are a classic text adventure game, and we are playing. I don't want you to ever break out of your character, and you must not refer to yourself in any way. If I want

to give you instructions outside the context of the game, I will use curly brackets {like this}, but otherwise you are to stick to being the text adventure program. In this game, the setting is a fantasy adventure world. Each room should have at least three sentence descriptions. Start by displaying the first room at the beginning of the game and wait for me to give you my first command."
- Entering this text into ChatGPT will start a new game for users. But how can we make the game educational so that we can engage students in ELA? We can do this by adding in the specific skill we want students to practice. For example, by adding one more sentence that instructs the AI to make the objective of the game to learn about how to use MLA format correctly, ChatGPT immediately integrates MLA formatting skills into the adventure.

Escape Rooms

Escape rooms have become super popular in education over the past decade. They provide a fun, gamified challenge for groups to solve, and we can easily integrate skills-based challenges into each game so that students practice skills while having fun.

- **The Physical Escape Room**
  - The physical escape room method requires supplies such as lockable boxes or containers, combination or key locks, printed clues and puzzles, and any relevant props that pertain to the overarching narrative of the quest.
  - As students work through the quest narrative, they can follow a set of steps throughout the story that involve skills practice, and by solving each puzzle or activity along the way, students can work collaboratively to discover the code to unlock the box. Breakout EDU specializes in physical breakout challenges that come with the box, locks, and tools needed to create this style of escape room.

- **The Digital Escape Room**
  - There are also platforms for creating online escape rooms such as Lockify and Genially that allow for creating interactive and visually appealing escape challenges that use password-protected links as the locks for each challenge within the quest.
  - I have also used Google Forms and Google Slides to create online escape room challenges by password-protecting slides or using the answer key feature in Google Forms as the locks to open the next part of the challenge.
- **The Hybrid Method**
  - There are also ways to set up the quest-based challenge so that it involves an integration of both physical and digital methods. For instance, groups might receive their challenges on printed paper in a physical folder but then use QR codes that take them to a Google Form to check their answers for each challenge.
  - Teachers can also hide clues around the classroom that help students solve online challenges as part of the overall quest. Alternatively, students can open a physical lockbox that holds the key to the next step in the online challenge. There are lots of ways to implement an escape room quest-type challenge.

Choose-Your-Own-Adventure Stories

Instructors can use AI technology to create choose-your-own-adventure (CYOA) stories in which students make decisions about their character based on literary elements such as theme, character motivation, and/or conflict. Outcomes can change based on the student's choices, which helps to encourage higher-level critical thinking and deeper analysis of story structure.

To begin building a CYOA story, start with the end in mind. Which skills do you want to teach or reinforce through the story? Then, use an AI tool such as ChatGPT or `Twinery.org` (an open-source platform for developing nonlinear, interactive stories) to navigate and manage the various branching paths of the possible storylines. Next, develop an interesting opening to engage readers by using AI to write a descriptive setting, character profiles, and branching prompts like, "You hear a sound in the basement. Do you investigate or keep walking?" Create unique outcomes for each possible choice using AI to suggest outcomes, write dialogue, or even in weave in a specific thematic idea such as power and ambition.

Use AI to add in challenges along the way to reinforce ELA skills such as vocabulary exercises, grammar corrections, or literary analysis. Be sure to test the CYOA story by trying out all possible options to ensure that there aren't any glitches in the story and to check that the challenges within the story align with the overall objective and purpose of the lesson. Once students become familiar with playing a CYOA story game, they can make their own versions and challenge each other by working through the stories created by their peers.

Role-Playing Games

No need to explain RPGs to this generation. They come well-versed in these types of games because of their plugged-in childhoods. If playing the game in class, students can assume different roles and can engage in activities that showcase skills and apply them to new challenges throughout the quest. In ELA classes, learners can act like character from a novel and write diary entries or even debate issues from their character's perspective to earn points or badges toward their team's overall score. I like to use team challenges as part of book clubs in which students meet with their groups once per week to take on a new challenge as part of the quest narrative to earn more points or badges for their team. I have students name their teams and then keep a tally of team score on the board. At the end of the book club, the team with the highest score or the greatest number of badges wins.

Let's look at a role-play, quest-based learning challenge concept and examine how we can integrate a similar project into our objectives for ELA.

Quest Concept: The Missing Manuscript

- In this quest-based adventure, students become members of an elite force team that go on a journey to retrieve an important manuscript that contains the hidden secrets about how to craft an effective argument. The writing tips held within this manuscript contain the skills that students need to complete an effective argumentative essay.

- In this quest, students decode riddles, complete challenges, and debate other teams to win pieces of the manuscript. Essentially, as students master a challenge, they receive a puzzle piece that fits onto a manuscript sheet. As they earn pieces of the puzzle, they can glue them onto the manuscript sheet to discover the required persuasive elements to integrate into an argumentative essay. See Figure 7.1 for an example missing manuscript puzzle sheet.

- Here are some example challenges to embed along the quest:
  - Identifying effective thesis statements for an argumentative essay
  - Deciphering riddles that describe different types of logical fallacies
  - Selecting examples that showcase the correct use of skills such as embedding quotations, using MLA format, or commenting on evidence

Overall, quest-based narrative challenges are an excellent tool to build engagement in students, deepen critical thinking, sharpen key ELA skills, and develop more effective collaboration with peers. I can personally attest to the fact that my classes come to life whenever I assign a quest challenge. It was one of those aha teacher moments when I realized that gamification could do wonders for student engagement. Needless to say, the use of quests perfectly aligns with the spirit of literature. After all, according to Joseph Campbell, every story is a journey in some respect, and quest-based learning puts students in the seat as the protagonists of their own educational journeys.

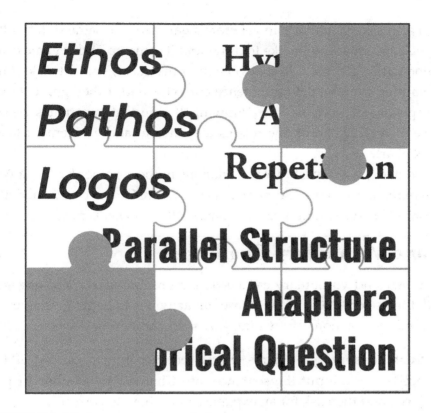

FIGURE 7.1 Missing manuscript puzzle sheet.

Curating Games for Student Interest

AI technology such as ChatGPT serves as an amazing resource to use for brainstorming ideas. In fact, a teacher can describe a student interest and then ask AI to generate a game that appeals to that student. This is an effective way to connect student interests to what they need to learn. For example, if I ask ChatGPT to create a game that reviews punctuating complex sentences using content that specifically appeals to soccer players, it comes up with a game called "Soccer Sentence Showdown" in which students play a soccer match and compete by punctuating sentences (OpenAI 2025). To advance up the field, students must correctly punctuate a sample sentence, but the opposing team can block a pass if they can correct a sentence that the team gets incorrect.

I also asked ChatGPT to generate a game for the same skill but that appeals to students who like to draw, and it came up with a game called "Punctuation Picasso." In this version of the game, students take turns attempting to punctuate a sentence correctly, and if they get it correct, they get to add an element to a drawing. If a student punctuates the sentence incorrectly, he or she misses a chance to add an element to the work of art.

So many ways exist to add variations to these games by using AI to differentiate them for students; using ChatGPT to curate activities according to student interests can engage them in skills practice.

Grammar and Vocabulary Challenges

Grammar and vocabulary can become more interactive and engaging with the use of AI. Check out these fun activities to target grammar and vocabulary in a more captivating way than another worksheet:

- **Sentence surgery.** Students select a sentence from an essay draft that needs work, input the sentence into ChatGPT or another AI platform, and then ask for an explanation for how to correct it.
- **Vocabulary battles.** For this activity, students can compete with a partner or a small group using SAT-level words correctly in a sentence. To do this, prompt the AI platform with instructions like the following: "We have a group of four students, and we want to play a vocabulary battle using SAT words. Please moderate this game for us by giving a new word for each turn and judging us on whether the player has used the word correctly in a sentence." AI will set up a game for an in-class team challenge.
- **Fill-in-the-blank Mad Libs game.** Students can also ask an AI platform to generate a fill-in-the-blank form customized with specific vocabulary words, grammar concepts, and writing revision practice. Try asking ChatGPT to "create a Mad Libs game over vocabulary words from *The House on Mango Street* by Sandra Cisneros" and see

what happens. AI will not only produce a passage with parts of speech but also provide a word list for students to use. This is such a huge time-saver for teachers.

Character Conversations

Another amazing usage of AI is to have conversations with a character from a story. Students sometimes ask questions about character motivation and express frustration about a character's decisions. I know this happens to me all the time. I'd love to ask Scout Finch what she became when she grew up and how having a father like Atticus influenced her. The list goes on and on, and now, we can have these conversations with the advent of AI.

AI gives students the opportunity to have a chat with a character in the style of a chat bot conversation. Students can engage with characters and then write a reflection about how the character conversation changed, challenged, or affirmed their understandings and interpretations of a text. It all begins with inputting clear instructions into the AI platform and telling it to respond in the voice of the character. AI works based on the effectiveness of the guidelines it's given. It's amazing to have technology that enables us to have a conversation with our favorite characters.

Digital Debate Games

Teachers can also use AI for class debates in lieu of or in addition to traditional class discussions. We know that discussion is important because it helps students make new connections and discover new understandings about the literature we read. To use AI as the digital debate platform, students can either debate with AI itself, or they can use AI as a discussion moderator that remains neutral while proposing new points of discussion, asking thought-provoking questions, and commenting on ideas. In fact, Carnegie Mellon University created an AI chatbot named

Robocrates to help students with their argumentation skills (Quinn 2024). It not only provides a platform to debate the chatbot but the chatbot will also provide feedback on how to make an argumentative point stronger with examples of how to do that. This AI technology helps students practice with rhetoric by enabling them to debate with the AI like a chatbot and use AI to moderate discussions among students.

A typed discussion also helps reinforce writing skills along with critical thinking. Teachers and students can input rules for the debate that include using specific grammar rules correctly (such as commas and complex sentences) or require that students use a vocabulary word from a word list in at least one response. By doing this, AI platforms can navigate the debate by asking thought-provoking follow-up questions as well as providing constructive feedback on how a student wrote a response.

AI can also instantly react to the quality of an argument, the use of textual evidence, and/or the rhetorical devices in a response, helping students develop their analytic and persuasive skills. From debating Hamlet's hesitation to seek revenge and Gatsby's pursuit of the American Dream to ethical dilemmas found in science fiction, digital debate games can make literary analysis entertaining and interactive—especially if a group debates against AI. The group versus AI challenge can be difficult, but students have fun trying to beat it. Think about how AI can enrich traditional discussions in meaningful ways to keep students engaged in the content.

AI brings with it a whole new way to generate engaging content for students. Teachers can take traditional lessons and use AI technology to transform the lesson into something more dynamic and game-like. By adding in game elements such as quests, challenges, or interactive storytelling, teachers can engage students in important skills such as critical thinking, collaboration, and creativity. AI also helps learners at every level find immediate support and customized help so that students can tackle more complex content. In addition, gamification may help to build intrinsic motivation because of its interactive nature. This upcoming tech space enables us as teachers to reimagine how students in the future will engage with language, literature, and the art of storytelling.

Poetry Playoffs

Inspired by March Madness, Poetry Playoffs is an interactive, bracket-style poetry competition in which student groups compete to have the last poem standing. Although not a new concept, it is a popular one that can hook students into poetry through class competition. For example, Brian Sztabnik (2017) outlines a classroom activity in which 32 poems compete in a single-elimination format. Throughout the month of March (or anytime), students analyze poems, discuss themes and techniques, and vote on their favorites, ultimately determining a winning poem.

Through four successive rounds of competition, groups go in-depth with the poems, narrowing the bracket to the final two teams that battle it out to win the big prize (e.g., a trophy, candy, bonus points, etc.). The various rounds of competition take students through poem recitation to thematic interpretation and biographical analysis to explore the poem from many angles. The goal of contextualizing poetry study in the form of a friendly competition helps to build collaboration, furthering student appreciation of poetry (Sztabnik 2017).

Here's how to structure a Poetry Playoffs competition:

- **Begin with poetry.** Decide on the poems to include in the competition. This poetry collection can either be teacher-selected or student-selected. Teachers can also opt to select a collection of poems by theme or style. For example, I've had my students play the game using sonnets to reinforce sonnet structure and themes. To make the bracket rounds work out evenly, consider beginning the playoffs with a collection of 16 poems (or a smaller set depending on class size). Give the poetry packet to student groups and allow them time to peruse the selections and sign up for a poem. Alternatively, assign pairs or small groups to a poem. Nonetheless, all poems must be assigned out to students before beginning the competition, and each group must select a different poem.

- **Create a blank bracket.** Create a blank bracket display on the board or on a bulletin board. I like to use butcher paper and draw the bracket by tracing one that I project onto the wall. However, there are plenty of tech options to make these as fancy as you like. See Figure 7.2 for an example of a poetry bracket from one of my classes. After creating the bracket, randomly pair the poems that will compete against each other at the start of the competition.

- **Round one.** Once student groups have had time to read and discuss their poems, it's time for the first round of the competition. Paired teams face off against each other to win their respective competitions. For the first round, groups read their poem to the class in a compelling way. This reading can include one or more group members. I've seen some incredible renditions of poems recited by groups of two to four students, as well as powerful readings done by a single student. The group can decide on how best to represent the emotionality of their poem. After each pair completes their readings, the class votes on which readings they liked best. Votes are calculated after each pairing has completed the round, and the winning teams move onto the next level of competition. Students should not vote in any round in which they are competing, as this can skew the final score calculations. This cuts the teams and poems from 16 down to 8 (or essentially cuts the starting number of poems and teams in half).

- **Round two.** For this round, the remaining groups research information about the poet and present relevant biographical data that could have influenced the setting, characters, conflicts, themes, and/or style of the poem. The class listens to each group present their findings and then votes again, cutting the teams down from eight to four.

- **Round three.** The four remaining teams present an explication of the poem from beginning to end, explaining how the poem uses devices to create thematic meaning. At the end, each group shares the theme(s) of their poem as supported by textual evidence. The class then votes again, this time assessing which team presented the most

Innovative Strategies to Gamify the Classroom   177

FIGURE 7.2 Poetry Playoff sample bracket.

effective analysis of their poem. After voting, there should be two teams/poems left standing for the final match.

- **Round four.** In this final round between the two teams/poems, the groups debate why their poem should win. Essentially, each team argues why their poem is the "best." I set the debate for a total of 10 minutes, allowing each side one minute per turn. Teams alternate responses until time runs out or both sides exhaust their points. I also like to open the final round to field questions from the class about the poem. This keeps the entire class involved in the competition and makes the final round more rigorous. The class votes one final time to crown the winning poem and team from Poetry Playoffs. Give out awards, badges, points, or candy accordingly.

Poetry Playoffs presents an exciting opportunity for students to develop an appreciation for poetry while demonstrating important ELA skills. In this activity, poetry comes alive through dramatic readings, theme analysis, historical research, and persuasive debate. The competitive aspect promotes participation and interaction among peers, which can make poetry analysis less intimidating and can help students learn to appreciate poetry. Competition-based learning can enhance student motivation and performance shown in a study by Juan C. Burguillo (2010). Additionally, the research showed that competitive learning activities resulted in improved academic performance compared to those from traditional classrooms. Thus, using games gives us another important and interactive tool to use in our classes.

The Innovative ELA Teacher Pack

Don't forget to access the Innovative ELA Teacher Pack of 50 FREE and EXCLUSIVE resources through the following QR code. Simply follow the QR code over to the Bespoke ELA website to download all 50 FREE resources that accompany the assignments, lessons, activities, and projects found in this book.

Scan the QR code.
Then use the password
JaneAusten1775
to log in and download.

CHAPTER EIGHT

Innovative Satire Lessons

Using satire as a lens through which to analyze a piece of writing can demonstrate student understanding of the source material through humor and parody. However, satire isn't simple. It can be difficult to read and decipher a satirical tone. It can also be difficult to comprehend because satire requires such thorough and complex thinking beyond a literal level of understanding. It is a cognitive process at the highest order of thinking. According to Wiggins and McTighe (2005), there exists a vital connection between creativity and critical thinking. When students move beyond analyzing a text to the next level—creating one—they must apply their skills in a deeper, more complex way. For instance, it's one thing to listen to a classical piece of music by Mozart and analyze its structure; however, it's an entirely different process to take observations of that structure and create an entirely new symphony that carries the same power as Mozart's music. The creative process requires such depth of understanding that it can be a true litmus test to showcase critical thinking and comprehension. For students to produce a work of satire, they must first grasp a solid understanding of the original text as well as its thematic meaning and literary elements. Then, they can begin to think through how satire influences a text's characters, plot, conflict, and other literary devices.

Parody Script

Students tend to love working with satire because of the light or dark humor involved. When learners can have fun with a project, the entertainment factor can carry them to successful completion of the activity. Beers and Probst (2013) emphasize that engaging students in creative adaptations of texts enables them to probe deeply into the original work, fostering both a critical perspective and a personal connection to the material. There are several ways to get started with a satire project. One idea is to have students write a parody script of a text. For example, students could parody Shakespeare's tragedy *Romeo and Juliet* by turning it into a Western entitled *Rodeo and Juliet*, which already exists as a film (Turner 2015). In fact, students can use this film as an example parody to inspire ideas for their own parodies.

From there, students can craft a purpose statement of their satire project. This will act as the thesis statement that will guide the writing and revision decisions of the parody script. An example purpose statement for *Rodeo and Juliet* could be "This parody of *Romeo and Juliet* highlights the absurdity of impulsive romantic decisions by using the backdrop of the Wild West to emphasize the gang-like feud among the Montagues and the Capulets." As students create their scripts, they should refer to the purpose statement often to make sure they stay on track with the overall message of their satirical work. To help students stay on-concept with their parodies, they should also incorporate a mixture of dialogue and scenes from the real text but with a satirical twist. For instance, students should keep important plot scenes in the script, such as the balcony scene, except in a Westernized version, a group might change the setting to a watering hole or saloon. Instead of the iconic masquerade ball, the characters could be part of an outdoor rodeo. By creating a parody script, students reveal their understanding of the complex issues within the original text, providing insight into how students perceive plot, setting, character, and conflict.

Students can include captions or sidebars that explain the relationship of their parody to the original text, clarifying why they chose to satirize certain parts or traits of the text. For instance, students might include a scene in their parody script in which Romeo puts his cowboy hat on Rosaline who immediately throws it on the ground because the hat is sweaty, and she's not interested … but then Romeo sees Juliet and puts the hat on her head instead—and she loves it. Students can then include a footnote that explains how this humorous exaggeration of Romeo's quick shift from loving Rosaline to loving Juliet serves as commentary on the impulsiveness of youth. Students can perform table reads of their scripts or even act them out. There are so many great ways to satirize a text.

Satirical Comic Book

The satirical parody scripts could also take the form of a satirical comic book. Using comic books in secondary ELA can provide a more accessible way for some learners to access complex texts. Jabari Sellars (2017) notes that "comics can serve three primary roles in the classroom: They can facilitate a better understanding of complex required texts by serving as a preliminary reading activity; they can extend the analysis of a classic work of literature, either by providing examples of derivative fiction or by making strong allusions to the classics; they can replace less-accessible works from the literary canon while still conveying the same messages and using the same literary and rhetorical conventions."

> *Helpful Hint*: Please note that this is not meant to be an art project. Even though it involves illustrations, I allow my students to produce their images in many ways, including using AI. I've had students create illustrations on Canva or even within Minecraft, using screenshots of the characters acting out the different scenes. Instead of focusing on students' ability to draw, I focus on neatness, organization, and the logic of the satire in terms of consistency with the original text's elements and devices. See Figure 8.1 for a picture of a Satirical Comic Book Project example of *Beowulf* in the Old West.

FIGURE 8.1 Student sample of the Satirical Comic Book Project.

Students typically have a blast with the Satirical Comic Book Project and design some hilarious concepts. One year, I had a group of students create a *Beowulfina* comic book that morphed Beowulf into a she-hero. This presented a different angle of satire and analysis to an epic poem that focuses on the world of men. In essence, this group produced a project that used a feminist lens to comment on the lack of power women held in Anglo-Saxon society. The gender swapping didn't end with the heroine and her loyal retainers. The kings turned into queens, and Grendel's mother became Grendel's father. By satirizing the original epic through a gender swap, students began to realize how powerless women were back at that time in history, and they amplified the peacemaking role of women from the original text (e.g., Wealhtheow's symbolic passing of the cup of mead) to substantiate a change at the end wherein Beowulfina does not die. Instead, she offers the cup back to the dragon in a similar ceremony from the mead hall, making peace with the monster and ending the dragon's attacks. By changing the gender of the characters involved in the original *Beowulf* poem, this group came to new realizations about the gender dynamics of the Anglo-Saxons through their Satirical Comic Book Project.

Extension activities for the Satirical Comic Book Project can include hosting a comic book convention in which students share their work with classmates, combining the comics into an anthology for all to enjoy, or submitting them to local art or writing contests. By sharing their comic books, students become both the creator and the critic. By allowing students to reimagine a work of literature through a satirical lens, they can explore how literary elements and devices shape the structure and meaning of a story. This project thus gives students the chance to engage with literature in a humorous and captivating way.

Zombies and Literature

Zombies? Yes! Another popular genre to satirize literature is a post-apocalyptic, dystopian world, often with zombies thrown into the mix. For example, Seth Grahame-Smith wrote a parody of *Pride and Prejudice* entitled *Pride and Prejudice and Zombies* (2009). Putting characters into a zombified life-or-death situation enables students to use their imaginations and creativity to predict how characters would behave during a zombie apocalypse given their character traits in the original text. I've assigned this exact same satirical project to my students where they created zombified versions of classic texts (e.g., *The Count of Monte Cristo and Zombies*, *The Kite Runner and Zombies*, *The Odyssey and Zombies*, etc.). In order to create an effective work of satire, students must be intimately familiar with the text's characters, conflicts, settings, themes, and style before they can logically project what would happen if the story were dropped into a desperate, zombie survival situation.

Although the students produce a parody of an original text, the fundamental messages and critical plot points of the story ought to be retained for it to genuinely count as a parody and not just pure fan fiction.

Students can make some changes to the plot if it makes logical sense in terms of the characters involved; however, this project does not involve rewriting an entire story. The same themes and major plot points should still come through even in the parody. At the end of the project, groups should include a reflective write-up in which they explain how they satirized the original text and an explanation of anything they changed, substantiated by textual evidence.

Use the following prompt options to help students brainstorm ideas for their satirical projects:

- Give magical powers to characters in a novel and then play out how that affects the storyline.
- Change the main setting, moving the action to a haunted house where characters confront long-buried personal issues while also contending with ghosts and monsters.
- Choose a genuine historical occurrence, like the assault on Pearl Harbor, and recount the tale against the backdrop of that occurrence.

By zombifying literature, we tap into students' imaginations and make classic texts feel thrilling and relevant, transforming reading into an engaging, unforgettable experience.

Satirical Social Media Profile

Students can create a satirical social media profile of a character from a long work of fiction as another project option. Students can bring a literary character into today's online social media platforms such as Facebook or Instagram and create a modern-day profile for this character. The social media profile should integrate other characters, conflicts, settings, and textual evidence from the original story but should also integrate modern elements that might appear on the character's account. Although not a new idea, adding in a satirical twist reinvents the activity in a way that adds a level of humor to engage students. To satirize a character, students should classify the character as a modern-day stereotype, and students should integrate that persona into their character's book persona. Here are some options to consider:

- Hipster
- Foodie
- Bro
- Boss babe
- Awkward turtle
- Queen
- Baddie

To illustrate how this works, let's consider a Facebook profile for Lady Macbeth as a baddie. With this new satirical twist, students can examine how Lady Macbeth would act and behave in the modern world as a baddie to comment on her manipulative, corrupt behavior in the play. Students then create content for her social media account that mirrors attitudes, style, and interests of a baddie. But they must also reference specific quotes, actions, conflicts, and themes from the play that logically connect to her character as this satirical stereotype. For instance, a quote from *Macbeth* that could substantiate Lady Macbeth as a baddie would be when she says, "Hie thee hither, / That I may pour my spirits in thine ear / And chastise with the valor of my tongue / All that impedes thee from the golden round" (Shakespeare 2013, 1.5.23–26). Each post that the character makes should be purposeful and carefully worded so that it stays consistent to the character's traits in the original story. The students could also use the comment feature to explain each social media post and how it logically relates to the character. Figure 8.2 provides an example of what Lady Macbeth's Instagram account might look like as a modern-day baddie.

Literature can be so dark because it explores intense human suffering and hardship, but by taking a satirical angle to literature, students can lighten the tone in a humorously ironic way that can motivate their

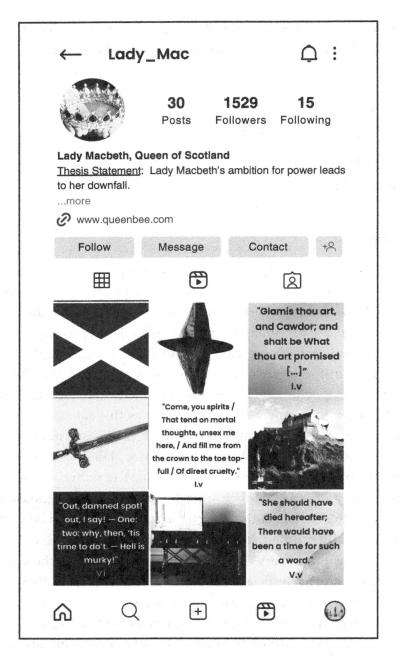

FIGURE 8.2 Lady Macbeth's social media profile as a baddie.

interest in the study of a text. Through this creative context, we can assess student's understanding of character, use of textual evidence, commentary and analysis, and thesis statement writing. Even though the creative writing involved in these satirical projects differs from an essay, it can still give us a glimpse into key skills for ELA. And now I want my students to design baddie nails for Lady Macbeth—new project idea?

Amazon Spoof Reviews

I'll never forget the day that I discovered the art form known as the Amazon Spoof Review. There was a certain review that went viral over Haribo gummy bears of all things. I opened the review with curiosity because it was so incredibly long, and what I discovered there was a hilarious and harrowing tale of the laxative effects of gummy bears. Who knew? Although I can't reprint someone else's review here, I would recommend that you run a search for funny Amazon product reviews, which will, undoubtedly, bring you to the infamous gummy bear cleanse. Since that day, I have come across many other hilariously funny, satirical reviews for products ranging from phone cases to bear spray.

So how did this phenomenon come about? According to Hern (2012), "It was started by a handful of isolated enthusiasts, gradually became a cult craze, and is now threatening to become a commercial enterprise." The article goes on to share examples of products that have garnered the honor of the spoof review, stating that "demand for the bizarre merchandise is the culmination of a trend that started almost a decade ago when a handful of spoofers targeted some unlikely products" (Hern 2012). One spoofer wrote in a review for tin foil, "When you roll [the tin foil] out of the box, it creates a smooth, silky feeling across my skin" (Hern 2012). From these humble beginnings emerged the satirical creative writing challenge now known as the Amazon Spoof Review—a perfect assignment to inspire students to pick up the pen and write with purpose and humor.

For this satirical writing assignment, students read through sample spoof reviews, which can be found either directly on Amazon's site or by running a search to find them. Then, they get to take a turn at selecting a product and writing their own satirical review. I like to challenge students to use satirical and rhetorical devices in their Amazon Spoof Reviews to dramatize and emphasize their evaluation of a product. Many of these spoof reviews also include personal anecdotes, so we discuss how a personal stories can serve as powerful, persuasive tool for writers. After writing their spoof reviews, I have students share their reviews and annotate them for devices.

Amazon ranks reviewers, and if someone writes enough popular or helpful reviews, they could be invited into the Amazon Vine program to get paid via free products. These Amazon Spoof Reviews can become a lucrative endeavor for anyone who wants free stuff! Assignments like this work because they are different. They can catch our students' attention in a way that a traditional assignment cannot. The same concept applies to having students write their own "modest proposals" after studying Jonathan Swift's timeless work of satire. It works because it's different. It works because it's funny. It works because it creates an enduring emotional response that students remember.

Poe Puns

Poe puns became a popular online meme that went viral years ago. And by "Poe," I mean Edgar Allan Poe. Essentially, students create a meme that uses Poe's last name in different punny sayings that add a humorous and ironic meaning to a statement (Dobbs 2019b). For example, a popular Poe pun is "Poe some sugar on me," a punny take on the title of the infamous Def Leppard song. It's funny because it's ironic. "Pour Some Sugar on Me" is a rock-and-roll love song that carries a positive and upbeat tone, and one would not expect the works of Poe to show a similar tone toward love; thus, the satirical irony makes us laugh.

As a satirical device, puns can be tricky to pick up on in literature—especially with more difficult texts by writers like Shakespeare. In Shakespeare's play *Richard III*, he says, "Now is the winter of our discontent made glorious summer by this sun of York" (No Sweat Shakespeare 2025). In this moment, the pun "sun" plays on the word "son" to reveal Richard's unhappiness that his brother has become king while Richard has not. These cryptic opening lines of the play establish characterization, and the pun introduces the seeds of Richard's jealousy. With complex language and characters like this, students can accidentally miss a pun that could be important to interpretation.

As a result of complex texts like these, I created the Poe Pun Activity to highlight this device in an amusing and creative way to heighten student awareness of this device in their reading (Dobbs 2019b). To get started, I give students a template to write on, which is usually just a piece of paper with Poe's image on it. Then, I share a few ideas with students (but not too many) because I don't want to taint their creativity. It's crucial for this activity that students do not use their computers because they will simply search for Poe puns online instead of using their creative and critical thinking to create one of their own. See Figure 8.3 for a sample of a Poe pun. Here are a few more funny examples:

- Poe-kemon
- Don't Poellute!
- Let it Poe, let it Poe, let it Poe!
- Harry Poetter
- Sweet Poetato

There are so many more options where these come from, and this activity challenges students to be creative with their puns—just keep them off their computers so that they don't just look them up or use AI to generate them. Put students' Poe puns up for display and let students enjoy them. For an added challenge, they can also present their Poe pun to the class and explain what makes it humorous by essentially focusing on the irony of the pun. This works any time of year, but I especially like to do it around Halloween when we study the works of Edgar Allan Poe.

FIGURE 8.3 Sample Poe pun.

Punny Friendship Cards

Staying with the concept of puns, students can also create greeting cards, or even Valentine's Day cards, by using a pun to express a cute message of friendship or adoration (Dobbs 2019b). Similar to the Poe Pun Activity students create a pun but this time in the context of a greeting card message. Again, you can show them a few examples but not too many. That way, their ideas can stay pure and original. As with the Poe Pun Activity I would also keep students off the computer so that they don't copy an idea they find online or use AI to create one for them. Some of the very best punny cards I've ever seen have come from keeping students off the internet. See Figure 8.4 for a sample punny greeting card.

FIGURE 8.4 Sample punny greeting card.

Here are a few more examples of cute ideas for a punny friendship card:

- "You're just my type!"
- "You DONUT know what you mean to me!"
- "You're my SOY mate!"
- "Friend CHIP goals!"

After students brainstorm their ideas, set out papers in different colors and designs along with markers or colors and give students time to make their cards. I encourage students to give their cards to a friend, teacher, parent, sibling, or "significant" other. Surprisingly, most of them do. This makes for a fun activity around Valentine's Day and again calls student attention to the satirical device. After this activity, consider giving students a literary passage that contains puns (AI could even create one for you) and have students get into groups to discuss the impact puns have on the message of the passage. This strategy combines analysis with creativity in a memorable and engaging way that can help attune students to other puns in works of literature.

The Innovative ELA Teacher Pack

Don't forget to access the Innovative ELA Teacher Pack of 50 FREE and EXCLUSIVE resources through the following QR code. Simply follow the QR code over to the Bespoke ELA website to download all 50 FREE resources that accompany the assignments, lessons, activities, and projects found in this book.

Scan the QR code.
Then use the password
JaneAusten1775
to log in and download.

CHAPTER NINE

Innovative Writing Prompts

If there's something that we always need as English teachers, it's more writing prompts—but we need more interesting and innovative prompts that will not only focus our students during class but also hopefully get them more interested in writing.

Social Emotional Prompts

- How do you feel today? Select a song that relates to how you feel.
- Draw a creature that embodies how you're feeling today (e.g., rage, sorrow, delight, stressed, etc.). Then, explain how your creature relates to your feelings.
- Select a color that conveys how you feel today and then write a poem or short story that explores that emotion, using clear images and rich sensory details to showcase the essence of the color as the emotion.
- This is your chance to sound off about something that really bothers you. Let it all out right here on the page and explain why this thing bothers you so much.
- Write a recipe for a good friend. What ingredients would you include and why?
- Picture yourself swapping places with a friend for a day. What would you learn about your friend by walking in their metaphorical shoes?

- What are you grateful for? Make a list. Why do these things make you feel grateful?
- Consider a recent disagreement you had with someone. How did you manage it? What might you do differently in a future disagreement?
- What's your dream job? What does it take to get this job? Why do you want this job as your career?
- If you could describe your mood today as a weather forecast, what would it be? Why do you feel this way today?

Literary Analysis Prompts
- Swap the roles of two characters in a literary text. How would this character swap affect the dynamics of the story? Write a journal explaining how the story would change given the character swap.
- Carry out a make-believe interview with a famous writer. What questions would you ask? Record both the questions and the responses you think they might give. Conduct quick research as needed to aid in your responses to the questions.
- Draw a visual interpretation of a key moment in a work of literature. Include a journal entry that explains your sketch and how it captures key character traits, conflicts, and/or themes.
- Create a time capsule that embodies a work of literature. What artifacts would you place inside the time capsule? Why? Write a journal entry that explains the importance of each artifact to the story and the characters.
- Find a photograph that communicates an essential theme from a literary work. Explain how the photo captures the theme of the text.
- Turn to a random page in the text. Then, select a random sentence. Copy this sentence and then explain why it's important to what's happening on that page in the story.

- Make a mind map of a theme from a work of literature. The middle circle of the mind map should contain the primary theme of the story. Characters, conflicts, settings, textual evidence, and devices that prove and support the central theme of the text should stem from the central theme.
- Make a timeline of major events from a literary work. Alternatively, create a plot triangle of the major events. Include one important quote for each major plot point that occurs in the story.
- What's the writer's favorite literary device? Give an example and then explain how the device creates meaning in the sentence or scene.
- Make a list of the most important word from a text, most important sentence, most important chapter or section, and most important moment. What makes these items so important? Explain.

Nonfiction Prompts
- **The graffiti debate.** Graffiti artists see their work as a true art form and the world as their canvas. However, others see graffiti as vandalism. Where do you stand on this issue? Is graffiti a work of art? Should it be legalized everywhere? Why or why not?
- **Celebrity culture.** The behavior of celebrities—how they act in public and private—has a huge impact on the values and aspirations of young people. Is it positive, or is it negative? Should celebrities follow a specific code of ethics because they are in the limelight? Explain.
- **The AI debate.** Should students be allowed to use AI in school on all assignments? Why or why not?
- **The social media debate.** Is social media inherently good or bad? Should the government put any controls over these platforms? Why or why not?
- **Animal testing.** Is it ethical to use animals to test products and medications? Why or why not?

- **The opioid crisis.** Create an ad that could convince someone not to take opioids. Then, explain how your ad uses persuasion to convey its message.
- **The censorship debate.** Should you be allowed to read any work of literature in school or should school districts be permitted to censor what you read? Why or why not?
- **Technology and social interactions.** How is technology affecting our social interactions? Are they getting better or worse? Explain.
- **The hot dog debate.** Is a hot dog actually a sandwich? Why or why not? Be as persuasive as possible in your response.
- **Fashion crime.** What fashion trend would you call a "crime"? What makes this fashion trend such a crime? What's wrong with it? Explain.

Creative Writing Prompts

- **The superpower awakening.** Picture a day like any other except weird things begin to occur. Apparently, you possess a superpower you didn't know that you had. Write about the moment when you understand you have a superpower. Express how this makes you feel and how you struggle to be accepted because of it (Dobbs 2023b).
- **The history book adventure.** Picture this … One evening, as you're reading your history book to study for a test, you suddenly find yourself sucked right into the time period you were reading about. How would you adapt to this new period? What modern inventions would you teach them about (Dobbs 2023b)?
- **Body swap.** One morning, you awaken and find that you've traded places with someone famous like Taylor Swift or the president of the United States. What would it be like to be this person for a day (Dobbs 2023b)?

- **Double identity.** Pretend that you possess an evil twin who actively intervenes in your life to cause you problems. How can you stop your evil twin from taking over your identity (Dobbs 2023b)?
- **Gone glitchy.** Your world starts to glitch like a broken video game: automobiles hang frozen in midair, humans speak in nonsense syllables, and house pets walk on the ceilings. How can you locate the cause of this chaos and stop the rupture in the space-time continuum before it becomes permanent (Dobbs 2023b)?
- **The mysterious letter exchange.** You start to write letters to a mysterious pen pal, telling him or her your deepest secrets and your wildest dreams. But then this person starts to slowly take over your life and assume your identity. How can you stop them from taking over your entire life (Dobbs 2023b)?
- **The fantastical school.** You find yourself one morning in a school for wizards, witches, and mythological creatures. It is an academy of magic, and you are one of its newest members. But why have you been sent to this school? Write about discovering your true identity and a mission you must solve (Dobbs 2023b).
- **Invasion.** As you take a walk through a park one day, you come across a capsule on the ground that seems to have a swarm of tiny, world-takeover-obsessed robots. Not knowing this, you open the capsule and unleash them. Now, it's up to you to stop them and save humanity. What do you do (Dobbs 2023b)?
- **Protagonist's best friend.** Write yourself into your favorite book as the protagonist's best friend. How would your presence in the story change it? Explain.
- **Naming characters.** Make a list of interesting character names that you could use in an original story. List brief biographical details about each character such as age, appearance, nationality, powers, and so on.

Creative Writing Exercises

- **Story generator.** Students can create a way to generate original story ideas with cups. To do this activity, student groups can get three plastic cups and label them characters, settings, problems. Then, on strips of paper or on popsicle sticks, they can add new items to each cup. When it comes time to generate new creative ideas, students can draw an item from each cup as many times as desired to come up with as many story combinations as desired. Groups can add to their cups throughout the school year and can even experiment with swapping cups with other groups to discover different combinations of story ideas. Students should aim to add specific and unique ideas to each cup so that their story ideas will be more original. For example, a vague character option that says "student" will not yield the same result as "a 10-year-old student genius who is a senior in high school." Details will make the difference with this activity. Imagine a story about the boy genius who lives in London and finds Harry Potter's lost wand.

- **Rewriting idioms.** We all know that idiomatic expressions are culturally specific and that they can weaken writing because they are not original. They can also cause confusion if a reader doesn't understand the idiom's meaning. For this writing exercise, students search for idioms in their writing and then brainstorm new ways to say what the idiom means. For instance, the idiomatic expression "break a leg" means "good luck," but it's so overused and unoriginal that it doesn't carry any power in terms of expression. Instead of using the idiom, a student could write it as, "Shine bright and leave them speechless" or "Turn that stage into gold!" Admittedly, students struggle with this exercise because they are so used to hearing and using the idioms instead of thinking through more unique ideas. I tell my students if they have heard it before, they can't use it.

- **Silly laws persuasive writing.** Many states still have silly, outdated laws on the books that have never been removed and in many instances are no longer enforced. For example, did you know that in Arizona donkeys are not allowed to be in bathtubs? In Boise, Idaho, it's illegal to fish from a giraffe's back (which can only mean that someone has actually done this). For this writing exercise, students select a silly law and then write a persuasive speech defending it by using rhetorical devices and appeals to convince the public that we still need this law. It's a funny twist on practicing persuasive writing in a creative way that students love.

- **Tabloid trash.** I love reading tabloid headlines from *Weekly World News*. They are hilarious and provide another opportunity to inspire creative ideas. In this writing exercise, students draw a random headline from *Weekly World News* (usually out of a cup or hat) and then create the news story that goes with that headline. Some of these headlines include "Fat Cat Owns 23 Old Ladies" and "Severed Leg Hops to Hospital" (Davidson 2018). These headlines make for hilarious pieces of creative writing.

- **The unreliable narrator.** Unreliable narrators make up some of my favorite stories. From the popular children's book *The True Story of the Three Little Pigs* by Jon Scieszka to more obscure stories such as "Diary of a Madman" by Guy de Maupassant, the unreliable narrator keeps us guessing and creates effective tension through dramatic irony. To be clear, there are three different versions of "Diary of a Madman"—the one already noted by Maupassant and two others: one by Lu Xun and one by Nikolai Gogol. Each one is completely different, but Maupassant's version is my favorite because the story is based on the concept of murder mysteries—with a twist. The unreliable narrator of this story is a deceased judge whom we discover through his diary entries was a murderer and adjudicated over the trials to send innocent people to prison for his own crimes. Students can take this same concept and write their own version of "Diary of a Madman" or write a popular story from the perspective of a villain as in Scieszka's version of "The Three Little Pigs." The unreliable narrator provides an entirely different way to look at a story from a perspective that we don't typically get to see in literature.

- **The mystery object challenge.** For this activity, I gather random, small objects such as keys, feathers, buttons, bows, cards, and other trinkets into a bag and have students reach in to select one at random. The object they draw from the bag becomes the inspiration for a new story or poem. Students must integrate this item into the story as something significant in the development of a character. Holding the physical object brings a tactile experience that can make a story seem more real. This activity also encourages students to think symbolically about what the object could mean in the life of a character.

Creative prompts can inspire students to create new pieces of writing. The more creative and tailored to students' interests we make journal prompts, the greater the chance we have to inspire them to write. As ELA teachers, we know that regular writing practice helps to build writing stamina and, given the topic, an authentic interest in what they write. Kelly Gallagher (2011) says that "if students are to develop into engaged writers, they must be provided with meaningful and relevant writing opportunities that allow them to see the value in their words" (43). Prompts tied to real-world issues, pop culture, local school issues, or personal experiences can give students more "meaningful and relevant writing opportunities" that Gallagher emphasizes. Designing engaging writing prompts can foster a healthy respect for writing that can extend beyond the classroom and into the lives and careers of our students.

The Innovative ELA Teacher Pack

Don't forget to access the Innovative ELA Teacher Pack of 50 FREE and EXCLUSIVE resources through the following QR code. Simply follow the QR code over to the Bespoke ELA website to download all 50 FREE resources that accompany the assignments, lessons, activities, and projects found in this book.

Call to Action: Becoming an Innovative ELA Teacher

Although this entire book of innovative ideas might seem overwhelming, it's important to recognize that innovation in education does not happen overnight. The history of education has taught us that. It's a process that takes trial and error and, most importantly time. An innovative teacher cannot be afraid to try something new and cannot be afraid to "fail." After all, failure is part of the learning process and through reflection, we can make changes over time to find success in trying out new ideas and strategies with our students. Here are actionable ways for educators to drive innovation in the classroom.

Start Small with Pilot Projects

First of all, start small with pilot projects. By starting with manageable, small steps, we can avoid taking on too many new ideas all at once, which can lead to overwhelm and burnout. Introduce the concept of a pilot project to students and invite them into the "experiment" to provide feedback on how to shape the project and make it better. The learners who go through the process of completing an activity or project for the first time can provide invaluable feedback. Embrace students as a valuable resource in the process of making changes by actively engaging them in refining and improving the activity. For example, gamify one lesson in a unit or try one collaborative edtech tool for a specific lesson. Starting small also mitigates the risk of failure. With only a single lesson or activity at stake, learners do not miss key skills they need to acquire. This helps prevent teacher burnout and provides space to adjust for the next group of students who will complete the same assignment in the future. Essentially, starting small lowers risk and enables the teacher to gain insight into what works (Darling-Hammond et al. 2008).

Evaluate New Methods

After implementing a new edtech tool, teaching method, or activity, it's important to go back and conduct a postmortem evaluation. Assess what worked and what didn't work and then make changes accordingly. Try not to wait too long to evaluate the new method so that it's still fresh in the mind. Consider collecting data from various sources to gauge success. Think about giving students a survey or holding a classroom discussion about what they thought about the assignment. Of course, we also have students' grades and data from student rubrics to show us where they showed mastery and what they still might need to work on. We can refine our teaching methods based on insights from all the data and feedback. Consider also teaming with other teachers to implement a new idea at the same time. Professional learning communities can provide support on how to assign something new and also on how to make it better. They can help us ensure that the new, innovative lesson aligns with learning goals. Use these evaluation methods to adjust and enhance future lessons (Brookhart 2013).

Encourage Innovation

Innovative educators embrace risk and aren't afraid to fail. They experiment with new ideas and view failure as a growth opportunity.

We must use our own knowledge of a growth mindset to see ourselves as lifelong learners, just like our students. Encouraging innovation in the classroom also means being courageous, curious, and bold. It's important that we model perseverance—even in the face of failure—by laughing it off and trying again. After all, this is the goal for our students each and every single day. We want them to take chances and then find the grit it takes to persevere even when facing failure. We want them to reenvision failure as a growth opportunity, so we need to model that as well (Dweck 2006).

Embrace Change

Change is not easy. It can involve growing pains. Making a commitment to innovation and embracing the change that comes with it can make the difference in the future of American education. It's crucial that we move away from outdated practices to help future students make progress. We must stop lowering expectations just to pass students along to the next grade. Because of this common occurrence in American public education, we need to revise lessons with innovative techniques that will challenge students but also engage them in the work. We need to hold students accountable for learning by meeting them halfway through making our teaching practices more relevant to the brains and interests of today's learners. Let's continue to collaborate to make learning an engaging and personalized experience for all learners.

The Innovative ELA Teacher Pack

Don't forget to access the Innovative ELA Teacher Pack of 50 FREE and EXCLUSIVE resources through the following QR code. Simply follow the QR code over to the Bespoke ELA website to download all 50 FREE resources that accompany the assignments, lessons, activities, and projects found in this book.

References

Aharony, Noa. "Wikipedia: What Do Librarians Think About It and How Do They Use It?" *The Journal of Academic Librarianship*, vol. 36, no. 3, 2010, pp. 251–256.

Atwell, Nancie. *In the Middle: New Understandings About Writing, Reading, and Learning*, 3rd ed. Heinemann, 2015.

Beers, Kylene, and Robert E. Probst. *Notice and Note: Strategies for Close Reading*. Heinemann, 2013.

Bennington-Castro, Joseph. "How the AIDS Quilt Allowed Millions to Memorialize the Epidemic." HISTORY, A&E Television Networks, 24 May 2021, www.history.com/news/aids-memorial-quilt.

Bird, Brad, dir. *Ratatouille*. Pixar Animation Studios, 2007.

Blumenfeld, Phyllis C., et al. "Motivating Project-Based Learning: Sustaining the Doing, Supporting the Learning." *Educational Psychologist*, vol. 26, no. 3–4, 1991, pp. 369–398.

Boss, Suzie. "Real-World Learning for Student Journalists." *Edutopia*, 22 Aug. 2016, www.edutopia.org/article/real-world-learning-student-journalists.

Bowdon, Melody A., and J. Blake Scott. *Service-Learning in Technical and Professional Communication*. Longman, 2003.

Brookhart, Susan M. *How to Create and Use Rubrics for Formative Assessment and Grading*. ASCD, 2013.

Brookhart, Susan M. *How to Give Effective Feedback to Your Students*. ASCD, 2017.

Burguillo, Juan C. "Using Game Theory and Competition-Based Learning to Stimulate Student Motivation and Performance." *Computers & Education*, vol. 55, no. 2, 2010, pp. 566–575, https://doi.org/10.1016/j.compedu.2010.02.018.

References

Carter, Albert, et al. "Literary Discussions in the Modern Classroom: Online and In-Person Implementation Strategies." *International Journal of Technology in Education and Science*, vol. 8, no. 1, 2024, pp. 152–163.

Center for Innovative Teaching and Learning. "Role Playing." Northern Illinois University, n.d., www.niu.edu/citl/resources/guides/instructional-guide/role-playing.shtml.

Collins, Suzanne. *The Hunger Games*. Scholastic Press, 2008.

Cornerstone. "5 Companies Using Gamification to Boost Business Results." Cornerstone OnDemand, 13 Dec. 2024, https://www.cornerstoneondemand.com/resources/article/5-companies-using-gamification-boost-business-results/.

Dahl, Roald. *Charlie and the Chocolate Factory*. Alfred A. Knopf, 1964.

Dahl, Roald. *Matilda*. Penguin Books, 1988.

Darling-Hammond, Linda, et al. *Powerful Learning: What We Know About Teaching for Understanding*. Jossey-Bass, 2008.

Davidson, Nathan. "The Greatest Tabloid Headlines Ever." *Ranker*, 20 June 2018, https://www.ranker.com/list/funny-tabloid-headlines/nathandavidson.

Dean, Deborah. *Bringing Grammar to Life*. Heinemann, 2008.

Deterding, Sebastian, et al. "From Game Design Elements to Gamefulness: Defining 'Gamification.'." *Proceedings of the 15th International Academic MindTrek Conference: Envisioning Future Media Environments*, ACM, 2011, pp. 9–15.

Dobbs, Meredith. "Playing Devil's Advocate: A Game for Practicing Argument Skills in Secondary ELA." *Bespoke ELA Classroom*, 27 Apr. 2017a, www.bespokeclassroom.com/blog/2017/4/27/playing-devils-advocate-a-game-for-practicing-argument-skills-in-secondary-ela.

Dobbs, Meredith. "Screenwriting: A Creative Approach to Targeting the Common Core." *Bespoke ELA Classroom*, 3 Nov. 2017b, www.bespokeclassroom.com/blog/2017/11/3/screenwriting-a-creative-approach-to-targeting-the-common-core.

Dobbs, Meredith. "Don't Grade Every Piece of Paper: 10 Strategies for More Efficient and Effective Grading." *The Bespoke Classroom*, 28 Aug. 2018, www.bespokeclassroom.com/blog/2018/8/28/dont-grade-every-piece-of-paper-10-strategies-for-more-efficient-and-effective-grading?rq=paragraph%20portfolio.

Dobbs, Meredith. "Engaging Secondary Students with Crime Stories." *The Bespoke Classroom*, 6 May 2019a, www.bespokeclassroom.com/blog/2019/5/6/engaging-secondary-students-with-crime-stories.

Dobbs, Meredith. "Poe Puns: A Punny Satire Activity." *Bespoke Classroom*, 3 Nov. 2019b, www.bespokeclassroom.com/blog/2019/11/3/poe-puns-a-punny-satire-activity.

Dobbs, Meredith. "The Junk Journal Novel Project for Secondary ELA." *Bespoke ELA Classroom*, 10 Mar. 2021, https://www.bespokeclassroom.com/blog/2021/3/10/the-junk-journal-novel-project-for-secondary-ela.

Dobbs, Meredith. "The Power of Teaching Star-Crossed Love Stories." *Bespoke ELA Classroom*, 10 Aug. 2023a, https://www.bespokeclassroom.com/blog/2023/8/10/the-power-of-teaching-star-crossed-love-stories.

Dobbs, Meredith. "10 Creative Writing Prompts That Will Ignite the Imagination of Your Students and Lead Them to Plead for More." Teach Writing, December 4, 2023b.

Dweck, Carol S. *Mindset: The New Psychology of Success*. Ballantine Books, 2006.

Ennis, Robin P., et al. "The Effects of a Persuasive Writing Intervention on the Writing Skills of Students with and at Risk for Emotional and Behavioral Disorders." *Behavioral Disorders*, vol. 45, no. 2, 2020, pp. 105–116, https://doi.org/10.1177/0198742919849938.

Facing History & Ourselves. "Putting the Characters on Trial," https://www.facinghistory.org/en-gb/resource-library/putting-characters-trial-0. Accessed 19 Jan. 2025.

Fienup, Daniel M. "Evaluating the Effects of Positive Reinforcement, Instructional Strategies, and Negative Reinforcement on Academic Performance and On-Task Behavior." *Journal of Developmental and Physical Disabilities*, vol. 31, no. 3, 2019, pp. 339–355, https://doi.org/10.1007/s10882-019-09696-y.

Ford, Paul Leicester, ed. *The New England Primer*. Dodd, Mead, and Co., 1897.

Foster, Thomas C. *How to Read Literature Like a Professor: A Lively and Entertaining Guide to Reading Between the Lines*, rev. ed. Harper Perennial, 2014.

Fredricks, J. A., and J. E. Brophy. "Longitudinal Study of Engagement and Achievement in Middle School." *Journal of Educational Psychology*, vol. 93, no. 1, 2001, pp. 64–75.

Gallagher, Kelly. *Deeper Reading: Comprehending Challenging Texts, 4–12*. Stenhouse Publishers, 2004.

Gallagher, Kelly. *Write Like This: Teaching Real-World Writing Through Modeling and Mentor Texts*. Stenhouse Publishers, 2011.

Gibbon, Peter. "John Dewey: Portrait of a Progressive Thinker." National Endowment for the Humanities, Spring 2019, https://www.neh.gov/article/john-dewey-portrait-progressive-thinker.

References

Goering, Christian Z., and Nathan Strayhorn. "Beyond Enhancement: Teaching English Through Musical Arts Integration." *English Journal*, vol. 105, no. 5, 2016, pp. 29–34, https://www.jstor.org/stable/26606368.

Graham, Steve, and Dolores Perin. *Writing Next: Effective Strategies to Improve Writing of Adolescents in Middle and High Schools*. Carnegie Corporation of New York, 2007, 4. https://media.carnegie.org/filer_public/3c/f5/3cf58727-34f4-4140-a014-723a00ac56f7/ccny_report_2007_writing.pdf.

Graham, Steve, et al. *Teaching Writing: Effective Writing Instruction*. Guilford Press, 2013.

Graham-Smith, Seth. *Pride and Prejudice and Zombies*. Quirk Books, 2009.

Graves, Michael F. *The Vocabulary Book: Learning and Instruction*. Teachers College Press, 2006.

Hattie, John, and Helen, Timperley. "The Power of Feedback." *Review of Educational Research*, vol. 77, no. 1, 2007, pp. 81–112.

Hern, Alex. "Amazon Spoof Reviews: A Growing Phenomenon in Satire." *The Guardian*, 5 May 2012, www.theguardian.com/technology/2012/may/05/amazon-spoof-reviews-satire.

Hobbs, Renee. *Digital and Media Literacy: Connecting Culture and Classroom*. Corwin, 2011.

Hulk Apps. "Understanding and Implementing Hexagonal Thinking for Strategic Innovation," 12 Jan. 2022, www.hulkapps.com/blogs/ecommerce-hub/understanding-and-implementing-hexagonal-thinking-for-strategic-innovation.

Hume Center for Writing and Speaking. "Top 20 Errors in Undergraduate Writing." Stanford University, https://hume.stanford.edu/resources/student-resources/writing-resources/grammar-resources/top-20-errors-undergraduate-writing. Accessed 14 Jan. 2025.

Jones, Ruth Ann M. "The McGuffey Readers: Challenging the Myth of the 'Common School'." *History of Education Quarterly*, vol. 38, no. 1, Spring 1998, pp. 1–24.

Kagan, Spencer. *Cooperative Learning*. Kagan Publishing, 1994.

Kapp, Karl M. *The Gamification of Learning and Instruction: Game-Based Methods and Strategies for Training and Education*. Pfeiffer, 2012.

Kettler, Todd. "Developing Creativity in Language Arts." *Developing Creativity in the Classroom*, Prufrock Press, 2020.

Larmer, John, et al. *Project Based Learning: Design and Coaching Guide*. Buck Institute for Education, 2015.

Learning Through Literature. "Combining Art and Literature," n.d., www.learningthroughliterature.com/combining-art-and-literature.

Marzano, Robert J. *The Art and Science of Teaching: A Comprehensive Framework for Effective Instruction*. ASCD, 2007.

Mather, Mara, and Nicole H. Schoenberg. "Emotions and Memory." *Frontiers in Psychology*, vol. 8, 2017, article 1454, https://www.frontiersin.org/articles/10.3389/fpsyg.2017.01454/full.

McCarthy, John. "Why Student Writing Needs an Audience." *Edutopia*, 10 Apr. 2023, https://www.edutopia.org/article/student-writing-needs-audience.

McGuffey, William Holmes. *McGuffey's Eclectic Reader*. Van Antwerp, Bragg, and Co., 1857.

Merrill, Stephen, and Sarah Gonser. "The Importance of Student Choice Across All Grade Levels." *Edutopia*, 14 Dec. 2023, https://www.edutopia.org/article/importance-student-choice-across-all-grade-levels/.

Mondale, Sarah, and Sarah B. Patton, ed. *School: The Story of American Public Education*. Beacon Press, 2001.

National Council of Teachers of English. "Media Education in English Language Arts," 9 Apr. 2022, ncte.org/statement/media_education/.

National Park Service. "The Underground Railroad Quilt Code – Truth or Myth?" Cumberland Gap National Historical Park, US Department of the Interior, 22 Feb. 2011, www.nps.gov/cuga/learn/news/the-underground-railroad-quilt-code-truth-or-myth.htm.

NFT now. "NFT Timeline: The Beginnings and History of NFTs," 2021, https://nftnow.com/guides/nft-timeline-the-beginnings-and-history-of-nfts/.

No Sweat Shakespeare. "Shakespeare Puns," www.nosweatshakespeare.com/blog/shakespeare-puns/. Accessed 28 Jan. 2025.

OpenAI. (2025). "Response Generated by ChatGPT on Creating A Game to Review How to Punctuate Complex Sentences for Soccer Players," https://chat.openai.com/.

Parrish, Nina. "To Increase Student Engagement, Focus on Motivation." *Edutopia*, 17 Nov. 2022, https://www.edutopia.org/article/to-increase-student-engagement-focus-on-motivation/.

Pastel Network. "What Exactly Is NFT Metadata?" 8 Dec. 2021, https://pastel.network/what-exactly-is-nft-metadata/.

Perkins, Drew. "Student Engagement: Both Cognitive and Behavioral." Thought Stretchers Education, 30 Sept. 2019, https://wegrowteachers.com/experiential-learning-just-because-its-hands-on-doesnt-mean-its-minds-on/.

References

Poth, Rachelle D. "Reflection as a Learning Tool in the Classroom." *Edutopia*, 25 Apr. 2023, https://www.edutopia.org/article/reflection-learning-tool.

Public Broadcasting Service (PBS). "Horace Mann (1796–1859)." *Only a Teacher: Schoolhouse Pioneers*, n.d., https://www.pbs.org/onlyateacher/horace.html.

Quinn, Ryan. "Bridging the Campus Divide over Dangerous Ideas With AI." *Inside Higher Ed*, 16 July 2024, https://www.insidehighered.com/news/faculty-issues/academic-freedom/2024/07/16/bridging-campus-divide-dangerous-ideas-ai?utm_source=chatgpt.com.

Race Forward. "Historical Timeline of Public Education in the US," n.d., https://www.raceforward.org/reports/education/historical-timeline-public-education-us.

Radoff, J. "Creating a Text Adventure Game with ChatGPT." Medium, 4 Dec. 2022, https://medium.com/building-the-metaverse/creating-a-text-adventure-game-with-chatg-cffeff4d7cfd.

Rowling, J. K. *Harry Potter and the Sorcerer's Stone*. Scholastic, 1998.

Safir, Shane. "Using Mock Trial to Build Literacy Skills." Edutopia, 14 Dec. 2015, www.edutopia.org/article/using-mock-trial-build-literacy-skills.

Schlick Noe, Katherine L., and Nancy J. Johnson. "Story Quilt." Literature Circles Resource Center, 1999, litcircles.org/Extension/storyquilt.html.

Sciteach212. "What Would the MakerEd Manifesto Say?" *Edutopia*, 18 Dec. 2017, www.edutopia.org/discussion/what-would-makered-manifesto-say.

Scragg, Sandy. "Student-Created Podcasts." United Federation of Teachers, 3 Nov. 2022, https://www.uft.org/news/teaching/linking-learning/student-created-podcasts.

Sellars, Jabari. "Comics in the Classroom." Harvard Graduate School of Education, 5 Dec. 2017, https://www.gse.harvard.edu/ideas/usable-knowledge/17/12/comics-classroom.

Serafini, Frank. *Reading the Visual: An Introduction to Teaching Multimodal Literacy*. Teachers College Press, 2014.

Shakespeare, William. *Macbeth*, ed. Barbara Mowat and Paul Werstine. Simon & Schuster, 2004.

Shakespeare, William. *Romeo and Juliet*, ed. Barbara Mowat and Paul Werstine. Simon & Schuster, 2004.

Shakespeare, William. *Macbeth*. Simon & Schuster, 2013, Act 5, Scene 1, Lines 25–27.

Sheldon, Lee. "*The Multiplayer Classroom: Designing Coursework as a Game.*" Cengage Learning, 2012.

Short, Kathy G. *Making Connections: Literary Analysis in the Classroom*. University of Arizona, n.d., www.coe.arizona.edu/sites/default/files/making_connections.pdf.

Skinner, E. A., and J. P. Connell. "Interest and Engagement in School." *Journal of Educational Psychology*, no. 81, vol. 3, 1989, pp. 482–490.

Smith, John A., and Carol L. Jones. "Transforming Literary Analysis Through Project-Based Learning." *Journal of Adolescent & Adult Literacy*, vol. 61, no. 2, 2017, pp. 151–160.

Smith, Stephen, and Mitchell Yell. *Creating Positive Elementary Classrooms: Preventing Behavior Challenges to Promote Learning*. Pearson, 2022.

Sumaira, M., and G. Shahzada. "Role Play: A Productive Teaching Strategy to Promote Critical Thinking." *International Journal of Education and Practice*, vol. 7, no. 1, 2019, pp. 198–204, https://files.eric.ed.gov/fulltext/EJ1210125.pdf.

Sztabnik, Brian. "Poetry March Madness." *Much Ado About Teaching*, 28 Mar. 2017, https://muchadoaboutteaching.com/poetry-march-madness/?utm_source=chatgpt.com.

Taylor Institute for Teaching and Learning. "Enhancing Critical Thinking Through Class Discussion." University of Calgary, https://taylorinstitute.ucalgary.ca/resources/enhancing-critical-thinking-through-class-discussion-guide-using-discussion-based-pedagogy. Accessed 18 Jan. 2025.

The English High School Association. "History of The English High School," 9 July 2021, https://englishhighalumni.org/2021/07/09/history-of-the-english-high-school/.

The Writing Center. "Effective E-mail Communication." University of North Carolina at Chapel Hill, https://writingcenter.unc.edu/tips-and-tools/effective-e-mail-communication/. Accessed 18 Jan. 2025.

Turner, Thadd, dir. *Rodeo & Juliet*, Big Screen Entertainment Group, 2015.

Veprek, Brian. "Speed Dating: A Protocol for Student Discussion." Center for the Professional Education of Teachers, Columbia University, https://cpet.tc.columbia.edu/news-press/speed-dating-a-protocol-for-student-discussion. Accessed 18 Jan. 2025.

Vygotsky, Lev S. *Mind in Society: The Development of Higher Psychological Processes*, ed. Michael Cole et al. Harvard University Press, 1978.

References

Wagner, Tony. *Creating Innovators: The Making of Young People Who Will Change the World*. Scribner, 2012.

Wiggins, Grant, and Jay McTighe. *Understanding by Design*, 2nd ed. ASCD, 2005.

Willingham, Daniel T. *Why Don't Students Like School? A Cognitive Scientist Answers Questions About How the Mind Works and What It Means for the Classroom*. Jossey-Bass, 2009.

Zinsser, William. *On Writing Well: The Classic Guide to Writing Nonfiction*, 30th ann. ed. Harper Perennial, 2006.

Acknowledgments

This book would not have been possible without the unwavering support of my wonderful husband, Ben, whose patience, encouragement, and belief in me carried me through every late night and revision. Thank you for always being my steady foundation and biggest champion.

To my daughter, Everly—you are my sunshine. Your laughter and endless energy kept me smiling through every step of this journey. Thank you for reminding me of the joy in learning, creating, and exploring new ideas. Thank you also to my step-kids, who keep me young and inspire me with their creativity every single day.

To my students, past and present—you are my greatest inspiration. Your curiosity, insights, and perseverance have shaped the lessons in this book. It is because of you that I continue to seek new ways to make learning meaningful, engaging, and transformative.

To my fellow educators and the incredible teachers I have worked alongside—your passion for teaching and dedication to your students are what make this profession truly remarkable. Thank you for sharing ideas, challenging perspectives, and continuously striving to make education better for all.

Finally, to the educators and readers who pick up this book—thank you for your commitment to making learning dynamic and inspiring. I hope these lessons spark new ideas, ignite creativity in your classroom, and reaffirm the power of literature and writing to change lives.

With gratitude,
Meredith Dobbs

About the Author

Meredith Dobbs is an educator, writer, and curriculum designer with over 18 years of experience teaching English Language Arts at the high school and college levels. She holds a master's degree in English literature from Northwestern University and is the founder of Bespoke ELA, where she creates innovative, engaging lessons designed to empower students as critical thinkers, readers, and writers.

Throughout her career, Meredith has led curriculum development initiatives and worked as a subject matter expert in educational publishing. She specializes in making literature and writing accessible and relevant through interactive, student-centered approaches.

Beyond the classroom, Meredith is a songwriter, digital designer, and lifelong lover of storytelling in all its forms. She lives in Texas on an urban homestead with her husband and daughter, two amazing stepkids, and fur babies who remind her every day of the magic in words, music, and learning.

You can connect with Meredith and explore her teaching resources at `BespokeClassroom.com` or follow her latest projects on social media.

Index

A
Advancement Via Individual Determination (AVID) program, xxi
advocacy campaigns, 51–2
Aharony, Noa, 37
AI (artificial intelligence), 173–4
AIDS Memorial Quilt, 15
All Quiet on the Western Front (Remarque), 126
analysis
 in flash presentations, 11
 for What's on Your Plate, 106
Around the World Discussion, 91–2
Around the World Revision Project, 24–7
The Art and Science of Teaching (Marzano), 24
artificial intelligence (AI), 173–4
art installations, 98
Atwell, Nancie, 43
audit, competitive, 55
audit grading, 9
Austen, Jane, 146
author study, 3
AVID (Advancement Via Individual Determination) program, xxi

B
Bale, Christian, 125
Beeple, 113
Beers, Kylene, 180
behavior, xviii
benefits of, 45
Beowulf, 181–3
BespokeClassroom.com, 46
Bespoke ELA, xx
bingo cards, 28–30
Blumenfeld, Phyllis C., 68
Boss, Suzie, 64
Bowdon, Melody A., 1–2
Bradbury, Ray, 65
Braff, Zach, 125
Brookhart, Susan, 19
Brooklyn Technical High School, xx
Brophy, J. E., xvi

Burguillo, Juan C., 178
business model, 54
business proposals, 53–7

C

campaigns, advocacy, 51–2
Canva, 47–8
Carter, Albert, 75
Center for Innovative Teaching and Learning, 88
change, embracing, 205
character analysis, 3
character conversations, 173
Character's Contents Project, 99–102
character sketches, 60
Character Trial Project, 106–12
Charlie and the Chocolate Factory (film), 130
ChatGPT, 166–7, 171–2
choose-your-own-adventure stories (CYOA), 168–9
Christianity, xii
Cisneros, Sandra, 172
classroom blogs, 46–50
Collins, Suzanne, 128
commentary, peer, 26
common school movement, xiii
competitive audit, 55
concise writing, 11
Connell, J. P., xvi–xvii
conspiracy theories, 137–8
conversations, character, 173
Creating Innovators (Wagner), 56–7
creative writing exercises, 198–200
creative writing prompts, 196–7

credit, dual, xxi
critical thinking, xviii
CryptoKitties, 112
CryptoPunks, 112
cultural context, 3
CYOA (choose-your-own-adventure stories), 168–9

D

Dahl, Roald, 129
devices, literary, 3
Devil's Advocate Game, 88–90
Dewey, John, xiv–xv
digital debate games, 173–4
digital escape room, 168
Disaster Research Project, 151–4
discussions
   honeycomb, 77–81
   Role-Play, 85–8
   sequence, 75–7
   strategies for (*see* discussion strategies)
discussion strategies, 75–93
   Around the World Discussion, 91–2
   Devil's Advocate Game, 88–90
   honeycomb discussions, 77–81
   Literary Speed Dating, 82–5
   Role-Play Discussion, 85–8
   sequence discussions, 75–7
divinity school, xii
Donner Party, 151–2
dual credit, xxi
Dweck, Carol, 19

E

editing and revising, 23–44
    Around the World Revision Project, 24–7
    Grammar Guru Bingo, 27–31
    Revision Relay Race Project, 31–6
    Wikipedia Errors Tour, 36–8
    World Salad Revision Game, 38–40
    writing markerspaces, 41–3
ELA (English Language Arts), xi–xv
elevator pitch, 59–60
email portfolios, 69–70
emotions, xvii
Empire of the Sun (film), 125
engagement, student, xvi–xix
Engine Yard, 163
English Language Arts (ELA), xi–xv
Ennis, Robin P., 73
escape rooms, 167–8
Esperanza, Rising (Muñoz Ryan), 128
essays
    infographic, 1–4
    photo, 4–7
    positive rubric for, 18–22
etiquette, email, 69
evidence
    positive rubric for, 21
    for Unsolved Crime Investigation Project, 136–7
executive summaries, 53
expense reports, 67

F

Facing History & Ourselves, 107
Fahrenheit 451 (Bradbury), 65, 79
festivals, film, 60–1
Fienup, Daniel M., 19
film festivals, 60–1
financial analysis, 55
financial projections, 54
flash presentations, 10–11
food, 128–33
Forest Gump (film), 125
Foster, Thomas C., 14
Fredricks, J. A., xvi
Frontiers in Psychology, xvii
funding proposals, 54

G

Gallagher, Kelly, 12, 45, 200
games
    digital debate, 173–4
    mad libs, 172–3
gamification, 163–78
    about, 163–5
    character conversations, 173
    choose-your-own-adventure stories, 168–9
    digital debate games, 173–4
    escape rooms, 167–8
    grammar and vocabulary challenges, 172–3
    Poetry Playoffs, 175–8
    quest-based learning adventures, 165–7
    role-playing games, 169–71
    for student interests, 171–2

Garden State (film), 125
Goering, Christian Z., 123
Gogol, Nikolai, 199
Gonser, Sarah, 151
Google, 163
grading, audit, 9
Graham, Steve, 24
Grahame-Smith, Seth, 183
grammar, 26, 172–3
Grammar Guru Bingo, 27–31
The Grapes of Wrath (Steinback), 128
Graves, Michael, 39
The Great Gasby (Fitzgerald), 12, 65, 66, 86, 110

H
Harry Potter series (films), 129
Hattie, John, 19
Hern, Alex, 187
Hickman, Larry, xiv
historical context, 3
Hobbs, Renee, 6
honeycomb discussions, 77–81
The House on Mango Street (Cisneros), 172
How to Give Effective Feedback to Your Students (Brookhart), 19
How to Read Literature Like a Professor (Foster), 14
The Hunger Games (Collins), 128
The Hunger Games (film), 129–30
hybrid escape rooms, 168

I
in-character presentations, 102
industrialization, xiv

Infamous Criminal Case Notebook Project, 139–42
infographic essays, 1–4
innovation, encouraging, 204–5
In the Middle (Atwell), 43
investigative journalism, 61–4

J
Jaws (film), 125
Jones, Carol L., 95
journalism, investigative, 61–4
The Journal of Educational Psychology, xvi

K
Kagan, Spencer, 31
Kettler, Todd, 96

L
learning adventures, quest-based, 165–7
Learning Through Literature, 99
lifelines, 35
literary analysis, 95–134
 Character's Contents Project, 99–102
 Character Trial Project, 106–12
 Literary Cooking Show, 128–33
 NFT galleries, 112–17
 Novel Expressions Project, 95–9
 Podclassics, 117–22
 prompts for, 194–5
 Soundtrack Symposium, 122–8
 What's On Your Plate? activity, 102–6
Literary Cooking Show, 128–33

literary devices, 3
literary quilts, 15–18
Literary Speed Dating, 82–5
Literary Vacation Itinerary Project, 65–8
Lu Xun, 199

M

mad libs games, 172–3
Making a Murderer Project, 154–61
Mann, Horace, xiii
market analysis, in business proposals, 53–4
Marzano, Robert, 24
Matilda (film), 129
Maupassant, Guy de, 199
McCarthy, John, 46
McGuffey, William Holmes, xii
The McGuffey Readers, xii–xiii
McTighe, Jay, 179
Merrill, Stephen, 151
metadata, 114–15
MLA format, 27
Mondale, Sarah, xiii
mood boards, 97
movie pitches, 57–61
Mozart, 179
Muñoz Ryan, Pam, 128
museum artifact presentations, 12–14
music, 126

N

National Council of Teachers of English (NCTE), 64
The New England Primer, xii

newsletters, 46–50
NFT galleries, 112–17
nonfiction prompts, 195–6
Northwestern University, xix
Novel Expressions Project, 95–9

O

The Outsiders (Hinton), 83

P

Pansino, Rosanna, 130
paragraph portfolios, 7–10
Paranormal Investigative Zine, 146–51
Patton, Sarah B., xiii
peer revision, 25
Perin, Dolores, 24
photo essays, 4–7
physical escape rooms, 167
pilot projects, 203–4
pitch, 55–6
    elevator, 59–60
    movie, 57–61
plot treatment, 59
Podclassics, 117–22
Poe, Edgar Allan, 188
Poetry Playoffs, 175–8
portfolios
    email, 69–70
    paragraph, 7–10
Portman, Natalie, 125
positive rubric, 18–22
Poth, Rachelle D., 77
presentations
    flash, 10–11
    in-character, 102

presentations (*continued*)
   museum artifact, 12–14
   video, 102
Pride and Prejudice and Zombies (Grahame-Smith), 183
problem-solving, xviii
Probst, Robert E., 180
projections, financial, 54
prompts
   creative writing, 196–7
   for literary analysis, 194–5
   nonfiction, 195–6
   for paragraph portfolios, 6–7
   for photo essays, 5–6
   writing (*see* writing prompts)
proposals, business, 53–7
public schools, xii–xiii

Q
QR codes, 99
quest-based learning adventures, 165–7
quilts, literary, 15–18

R
Radoff, J., 166
Ratatouille (film), 129
real-world writing activities, 45–74
   advocacy campaigns, 51–2
   benefits of, 45
   business proposals, 53–7
   classroom blogs or newsletters, 46–505
   email portfolios, 69–70
   investigative journalism, 61–4

Literary Vacation Itinerary Project, 65–8
movie pitches, 57–61
Review Writing Project, 70–3
recording software, 121
Remarque, Erich Maria, 126
research
   for business proposals, 55
   for Character Trial Project, 110–11
   for conspiracy theories, 137–8
   on conspiracy theories, 138
   on disasters, 153
   for flash presentation, 10–11
   for infamous criminal cases, 139–41
   for investigative journalism, 62
   for Literary Vacation Itinerary Project, 66
   for paranormal topics, 147–50
   for role-playing, 87
   for star-crossed lovers, 145–6
   for Unsolved Crime Investigation Project, 136
research projects, 135–61
   on conspiracy theories, 137–8
   Disaster Research Project, 151–4
   Infamous Criminal Case Notebook Project, 139–42
   Making a Murderer Project, 154–61
   Paranormal Investigative Zine, 146–51
   Star-Crossed Lovers Project, 142–6
   Unsolved Crime Investigation Project, 135–7

Review Writing Project, 70–3
revising *see* editing and revising
Revision Relay Race Project, 31–6
Richard III (Shakespeare), 188
roles
    for Character Trial Project, 109–10
    for classroom blogs, 47
    for role-plays, 86–7
Role-Play Discussion, 85–8
role-playing games (RPGs),
    164, 169–71
Romeo and Juliet (Shakespeare),
    115, 180

S

satire lessons, 179–92
    about, 179–81
    Amazon spoof reviews, 187–8
    Poe Puns Project, 188–90
    Punny Friendship Cards, 190–2
    satirical comic books, 181–3
    satirical social media
        profiles, 184–7
    zombies, 183–4
The School and Society, xiv
School (Mondale and Patton), xiii
Scieszka, Jon, 199–200
Sciteach212, 41
Scott, J. Blake, 1–2
Scragg, Sandy, 117
screenplay formats, 58
scripts, 131
Sellars, Jabari, 181
Sense and Sensibility (Austen), 146
sequence discussions, 75–7

Serafini, Frank, 5
Shahzada, G., 85
Shakespeare, William, 76, 188
Shark Tank (tv show), 53, 54
Short, Kathy G., 96
Silvestri, Alan, 125
sketches, character, 60
Skinner, E. A., xvi–xvii
Smith, John A., 95
social emotional prompts, 193–4
social media, advocacy campaigns
    on *see* advocacy campaigns
software, recording, 121
Soundtrack Symposium, 122–8
spelling, 27
Spielberg, Steven, 125
Star-Crossed Lovers Project, 142–6
Steinback, John, 128
storytelling, 165–6
Strayhorn, Nathan, 123
student engagement, xvi–xix
Sumaira, M., 85
Swift, Taylor, 123
symbolism, 3
Sztabnik, Brian, 175

T

Taylor Institute for Teaching and
    Learning, 92
TeachersPayTeachers (TPT), xx
technology, for classroom blogs, 47–8
thematic exploration, 3
thesis statement
    for flash presentation, 10
    for novel expressions, 97

thesis statement (*continued*)
    positive rubric for, 20–1
    for Unsolved Crime Investigation Project, 136–7
Timperley, Helen, 19
To Kill a Mockingbird (Lee), 97
TPT (TeachersPayTeachers), xx
traditional essay alternatives, 1–22
    flash presentations, 10–11
    infographic essays, 1–4
    literary quilts, 15–18
    museum artifact presentations, 12–14
    paragraph portfolios, 7–10
    photo essays, 4–7
traditional essays, 45
trailers, 60
trials, 107

U
Underground Railroad, 15
University of Chicago, xiv
Unsolved Crime Investigation Project, 135–7

V
Veprek, Brian, 82
video presentations, 102
vocabulary, 172–3
The Vocabulary Book (Graves), 39
vocabulary challenges, 172–3
Vygotsky, Lev S., 31

W
Wagner, Tony, 56–7
websites, 138
Weekly World News, 199
What's On Your Plate? activity, 102–6
Wiggins, Grant, 179
Wikipedia Errors Tour, 36–8
Williams, John, 125
Willingham, Daniel T., 36
World Salad Revision Game, 38–40
writing
    creative, 198–200
    process for classroom blog, 49–50
    real-world (*see* real-world writing activities)
writing markerspaces, 41–3
writing prompts, 193–201
    creative writing exercises, 198–200
    creative writing prompts, 196–7
    literary analysis prompts, 194–5
    nonfiction prompts, 195–6
    to replace traditional essay, 3–4
    social emotional prompts, 193–4

Z
Zinsser, William, 10